D0399409

BREAKING FREE
DAY BY DAY

A YEAR OF WALKING IN LIBERTY

Beth Moore

BREAKING FREE

DAY BY DAY

B&H
PUBLISHING GROUP

NASHVILLE TENNESSEE

Breaking Free Day by Day:
A Year of Walking in Liberty

ISBN 978-0-8054-4646-3
B&H Publishing Group
Nashville, Tennessee
www.BHPublishingGroup.com

Dewey Decimal Classification: 248.84
Freedom (Theology) \ Christian Life \ Bible O.T.
Isaiah–Study

Printed in China
1 2 3 4 5 10 09 08 07

DEDICATION

To the wonderful people of
Franklin Avenue Baptist Church,
my home away from home.
I will never be able to think about
the message of *Breaking Free*
without thinking of you.
Words are inadequate to express
my gratitude for your loving
share in this vision. You have
stolen my heart.

THE SPIRIT OF THE LORD
GOD IS ON ME, BECAUSE
THE LORD HAS ANOINTED
ME TO BRING GOOD NEWS
TO THE POOR. HE HAS
SENT ME TO HEAL THE
BROKENHEARTED, TO
PROCLAIM LIBERTY TO THE
CAPTIVES, AND FREEDOM
TO THE PRISONERS.

Isaiah 61:1

Introduction

Welcome to *Breaking Free*.

I have never written anything that meant more to me than the message of this book. And because this volume is so precious to me, I desperately desire for it to be precious to you.

When I was eighteen, I surrendered to God's call to vocational ministry. Some years later, God spoke to my heart and said something like this: "I sent my Son to set the captives free. You will go forth and ring the liberty bell." Sweet thought. Even a little poetic for a romantic like me, but it sounded awfully evangelistic for a young woman like me who was fairly certain her calling was in the area of discipleship.

Oh, how could I have thought that the only people held captive in this generation were the spiritually lost? To confirm this fact, God proceeded to work on my own heart from the inside out. I had no idea I was in captivity myself until God began to set me free.

That's why today I am desperate for you and for your freedom. I long for you to join the unshackled multitude that is breaking free!

As we launch out on this year together, I need to challenge you. We will consider many biblical keys to liberty in the days ahead, but don't expect to find a magic potion inside. Real freedom requires real work. And a key part of this work involves God's Word. We need to hide His Word in our heart so that we might not sin against Him (Ps. 119:11).

So I urge you not to skip lightly over the Bible verses that introduce each day's short reading. These Scriptures are crucial! You need to read them, meditate on them, and look them up in your own Bible to study the context from which they come. I believe God's Word brings freedom—His incarnate Word through His written Word.

Here's some of what we'll discover this year. We'll see how captivity came to the kings and people of ancient Israel—and how true freedom comes through the King of kings.

We'll encounter the benefits of the Christian life that make freedom possible. We'll see how the Father intends benefits for every one of His children, and we'll pinpoint the major obstacles that block the way to that freedom.

I'll ask you at times to take a look back at your life, knowing that in facing some ancient ruins and broken hearts, you will begin to find the freedom God promises. We'll see how strongholds take such deep root in believers' lives. But we'll also see that God wants to surpass our best dreams, bringing us into a place of obedience that really lasts, into a love that will not fade or fail, and into a genuine freedom that can grow only in the light of His unfailing love.

This is the promise of God for you, to be discovered and experienced *Day by Day*.

January

This is the land I promised Abraham,
Isaac, and Jacob, "I will give it
to your descendants."
Deuteronomy 34:4

Like Moses, we will scale the heights
this year to gaze over into the promised
land, the land of freedom and splendor.
But unlike Moses, we will have the opportunity not only to see it but to cross over
and live there.

So come with all haste. Come to the
place of breaking free. The place where
we truly know God and believe Him. The
place where we seek His glory and forget
our own. The place where satisfaction
comes from the only true satisfier of our
souls. The place where we experience His
peace no matter what the world may
throw our way. The place where His presence is our constant desire and daily joy.

> For I satisfy the thirsty person
> and feed all those who are weak.
> *Jeremiah 31:25*

Can you think of anything you've worked hard to attain that ultimately failed to bring you the satisfaction you expected? We can easily be led into captivity by seeking other answers to needs and desires that only God can meet. Perhaps we each have experienced an empty place deep inside that we tried our best to ignore or to fill with something other than God.

A crucial part of fleshing out our liberation in Christ means allowing Him to fill the empty places in our lives. Satisfaction in Christ can be a reality. He can make us feel complete. I'm not talking about a life full of activity. I'm talking about a soul full of Jesus.

My body faints for You in a land
that is dry, desolate, and without water.

Psalm 63:1

What do you usually do when you're hungry or thirsty? You seek what will meet your need. If you ignore your physical needs long enough, not only will you be miserable; you will be ill.

You can easily recognize the signals your body gives for food and nourishment, but great wisdom lies in learning how to discern the signals your spiritual nature gives. The most obvious symptom of a soul in need of God's satisfaction is a sense of inner emptiness—the awareness of a "hollow place" somewhere deep inside—the inability to be satisfied. Let this longing drive you to your Savior.

There will be times of security
for you—a storehouse of salvation,
wisdom, and knowledge.
Isaiah 33:6

Obedient lives flow from obedient days, and victorious lives flow from victorious days. Likewise, constructive lives flow from constructive days, built on the sure foundation of Jesus Christ.

When was the last time you felt that everything in your life was quaking except your stability in Christ? I love the thought of God's being our stability, don't you? Words to a familiar hymn ring in my soul: "On Christ the Solid Rock, I stand / All other ground is sinking sand / All other ground is sinking sand." God's benefits include the daily treasures of His strength and a sure foundation.

The Lord will not forsake His people
or abandon His heritage.
Psalm 94:14

Anything passed down to us through our family heritage that inhibits the full expression of freedom we should have in Christ qualifies as bondage. These yokes can be caused by severed relationships, lives left in ruins because of a loss or tragedy, or ancient family arguments and inheritances of hate. We need to examine areas of devastation or defeat that have been in our family lines for generations.

But be assured that the cross of Calvary can set you free from every yoke. His Word can make liberty a practical reality, no matter what those who came before you left as an "inheritance."

> The imperishable quality of a
> gentle and quiet spirit . . . is very
> valuable in God's eyes.
>
> *1 Peter 3:4*

How thankful I am for the freedom God has increasingly given me in Christ. I'm in the throes of middle age—(as one of my friends says, "Time is a great healer but a lousy beautician")—yet I am happier and more satisfied than I've ever been. The secret? I'm learning to see myself as beautiful to Christ.

Without Christ, every woman has intense insecurities. Unless we find our identity in Him, we Christian women can be just as prone to insecurities about our appearance as unbelievers. To Christ, the most beautiful person on earth is the one making preparation to meet the Groom.

I urge you to present your bodies as a living
sacrifice, holy and pleasing to God.

Romans 12:1

To be liberated in Christ, we've got
some sacrifices to make. And as long as
He is the one asking us for them—not our
own guilt or legalistic tendencies—any
sacrifice we make in our quest for freedom
will be wholly consumed by God as a
sweet sacrifice. He will bless it.

We fear making sacrifices. But the
irony is that we also make a lot of sacrifices when we are *not* living in the will of
God. How many things have we placed
on the altar to Satan's kingdom? Don't we
live sacrificially when we're outside the
will of God, giving up all sorts of things
that were meant to be ours in Christ?

> He returned to Israel's camp and said,
> "Get up, for the Lord has handed
> the Midianite camp over to you."
> *Judges 7:15*

God wants to remove all your doubts concerning who brings the victory in your life. He did this dramatically with Gideon. You probably know the historical account of how he assembled his army. The enemy numbers were like locusts, but God said Gideon's army was too big. So God took Gideon through the world's first reduction-in-force. He reduced Gideon's army from 32,000 to 300 men.

In the same way, no amount of determination will bring us freedom. We learn to be victorious by surrendering our lives completely to the Spirit of God, not by gritting our teeth and trying harder.

I, the Lord your God, hold your right hand
and say to you, "Do not fear, I will help you."
Isaiah 41:13

It's okay with God for you to be scared
to death. He recognizes our fears and our
insecurities. I feel like the Spirit of God
sometimes says to me, "You know, Beth, I
understand that you're not very happy
about this. I understand that you may be
crying over this. Cry, shake, whatever—
but do My will, child. Do My will. I have
victory for you."

So even though you may be afraid
about many things, don't be afraid to
allow God to do His work in you, looking
into the deepest part of your heart and
releasing freedom in your life, teaching
you how to live in victory.

Give glory to the Lord your God
before He brings darkness, before your feet
stumble on the mountains at dusk.
Jeremiah 13:16

Judah's King Uzziah might have been remembered as the greatest king between David and Christ except for one thing: the sin of pride became his downfall. He usurped a role saved exclusively for the priests, taking on the forbidden task of burning incense in the holy place within the temple of God. As a result, God struck Uzziah with leprosy. He had been a good man, yet when his life was over, all people could say was, "He had leprosy."

Pride can lead to captivity. It becomes an obstacle every believer must face on the freedom trail. What will you learn from the downfall of others?

> Humble yourselves before the Lord,
> and He will exalt you.
>
> *James 4:10*

Not long ago, I decided to purchase a new Bible. My old one looked like someone had put it in the dishwasher on "pot scrubber." I told my coworkers that I was going to keep the new Bible at work until I could get accustomed to it and still take my old one on speaking engagements.

As the words came out of my mouth, the Holy Spirit seemed to whisper in my ear, "Sounds like pride to me." He was right. I didn't want to have to struggle to find Scriptures in front of a group. Truly, the most effective means the enemy has to keep believers from being full of the Spirit is to keep us full of ourselves.

> This is love: that we walk
> according to His commands.
> *2 John 6*

How does liberty in Christ become a reality in life? *Obedience!* Obedience to God's Word. Rightly responding to the Word of God is our ticket on the freedom train. God's Word is the perfect law that gives freedom.

I know that sometimes we can be in too much bondage to even imagine living an obedient life. We want God to some-how wave a wand over us and magically remove every hindrance without requiring anything of us. But if God simply waved a wand over us and broke every yoke with-out our cooperation, we would soon pick up another. We cannot go forward with-out obedience.

He is always able to save those who
come to God through Him, since He
always lives to intercede for them.
Hebrews 7:25

If our liberty in Christ is going to be a
reality in life, we are going to have to learn
to walk in the freedom of Christ, independent of everyone else we know. We are
going to have to walk with Him alone.

That's because we need more than a
human leader on our road to freedom. We
need a Savior—One who keeps on saving.
If you're like me, you can think of more
than a few potential disasters from which
Christ has saved you since your initial
experience of salvation. Although we need
to be saved only once from being eternally
separated from God, Christ continues His
saving work in us the rest of our lives.

This is My Son, the Chosen One; listen to Him.
Luke 9:35

Long before a certain visionary had "discovered" the earth was round, God sat enthroned above the circle of the earth. Long before the first billion dollars was invested in exploring space, God's own hands stretched out the heavens. Long before there was a "beginning," God had already planned the end.

Sometimes what we need to cure our fat egos is a strong dose of God. Like Peter on the mount of transfiguration, we can get so wrapped up in ourselves and in the tabernacles we want to build that we miss a fresh revelation of God's glory right before our eyes.

If anyone walks during the day, he doesn't stumble, because he sees the light of this world.

John 11:9

If we were able to go back and look at the footprints of our life, we'd see that sometimes we went back to look at old resentments and habits. Sometimes we chose our own path or wandered onto another person's path we liked better. At other times we simply stopped because we couldn't let go of something that we couldn't take with us.

"But Father, we ended up okay even if I didn't walk with You every single day, didn't we?" He holds you close to His side and smiles, "Yes, child, we ended up okay. But you see, 'okay' was never all I had in mind for you."

For the wages of sin is death, but the gift of God
is eternal life in Christ Jesus our Lord.

Romans 6:23

We have exactly two options: we can
be slaves to a loving God or slaves to sin.
Door number three only exists on *Let's
Make a Deal.* Because we are creatures,
we are going to be mastered; the question
becomes, "Who will be our master?"

But does this mean we must obey God
simply because He is in charge? Actually,
my primary motivation for pursuing the
obedient life in Christ is an absolute belief
that the One who has the right to rule is
also the One whose rule is right. With all
my heart I believe God is always good,
always right, and loves me in ways I
cannot comprehend.

A thief comes only to steal and to kill
and to destroy. I have come that they may
have life and have it in abundance.
John 10:10

I believe practically every little girl has at least four dreams: 1) to be a bride, 2) to be beautiful, 3) to be fruitful (which we usually define as having children), and 4) to live happily ever after.

Boys have dreams that don't differ all that much. They also want a significant relationship and want to be considered handsome. Boys desire a legacy, and they certainly want to live happily ever after.

But while Satan desires to destroy our dreams, God wants to surpass them. He gives us our dreams so we'll long for His reality.

I have observed the misery of My people
in Egypt, and have heard them crying out
because of their oppressors.

Exodus 3:7

God hears the cry of the oppressed.
He even hears the cries of those whose
oppression is a result of sin and rebellion.
We must never cease believing that God
cares about those in physical, emotional,
mental, or spiritual prisons. He cares more
for our freedom than even we do.

Whether the Israelites fell victim to
their taskmasters in Egypt or walked in
slavery because of disobedience and idolatry, God had deliverance in mind for them.
As long as the sun comes up in the morning, God will keep offering to deliver His
children.

They will tremble with awe because
of all the good and all the peace
I will bring about for them.
Jeremiah 33:9

God does not minimize the things that break our hearts. He is not looking down on us, thinking how petty we are because things have hurt us. If we are so "heavenly minded" that we grow out of touch with earthly hardships, we've missed an important priority of Christ. God left our bare feet on the hot pavement of earth so we could grow through our hurts, not ignore and refuse to feel our way through them.

So surrender your hurt to Him, withholding nothing, and invite Him to work miracles from your misery. Be patient and get to know Him through the process of healing.

> He has sent Me to heal the brokenhearted,
> to proclaim liberty to the captives.
> *Isaiah 61:1*

When I think of bondage, I most often imagine yokes that come from some area of childhood trauma or victimization, because the yoke formed in my childhood has been the primary area of captivity I've had to combat. Most of us unknowingly limit our perceptions of captivity to those bonds we've personally experienced.

But Christ came to set the captive free no matter what kind of yoke binds them. He came to bind up the brokenhearted no matter what broke the heart. He came to open the eyes of the blind no matter what veiled the vision.

What has never come into a man's
heart is what God has prepared
for those who love Him.
1 Corinthians 2:9

Are you experiencing the benefits of
your covenant relationship with God
through Christ, or do the benefits you
read about in Scripture seem more like
warm, fuzzy thoughts? God has graciously
extended these five benefits to us:

1) To know God and believe Him
2) To glorify God
3) To find satisfaction in God
4) To experience God's peace
5) To enjoy God's presence

These five benefits will serve as a road
map to lead you home any time you've
been carried away captive.

How happy you are, Israel!
Who is like you, a people saved by the Lord?
Deuteronomy 33:29

I fear we may have become so legalistic in many of our Christian circles that we've dropped the word *happy* from our "religious" vocabulary. But sometimes God just plain makes me HAPPY! Call me immature, but picture me smiling.

Sure, I know that people are starving on the other side of the world. I'm deeply concerned for hurting people, and I pray for other nations every single day. But I also enjoy a happy moment in Jesus when it comes. Happiness is inappropriate when it's our goal, but not when it's God's momentary gift to us. Open it. Enjoy it. And remember it when times get tough.

For I am God, and there is no other;
I am God, and no one is like Me.

Isaiah 46:9

We make life so much more compli-
cated when we think life is "all about us."
The rest of the world never cooperates.
No one else got the memo. When we see
ourselves as the center of the universe, we
live in constant frustration because the
rest of creation refuses to revolve around
us.

Life vastly simplifies, and satisfaction
greatly amplifies, when we begin to realize
our awesome roles. God is God. From our
perspective, it's all about Him. He is the
center of the universe. We seek to please
Him. He seeks to perfect us—and life
works. Not without pain, but definitely
with purpose.

> Happy are the people who know
> the joyful shout; Lord, they walk
> in the light of Your presence.
> *Psalm 89:15*

When my sweet daddy had a stroke, I rode with him in the ambulance. The paramedics were wonderful and, although I appreciated what they did in our period of crisis, we didn't trade phone numbers or plan to have lunch.

Sometimes we approach God the same way. He gets us through an emergency, and we appreciate it. But we don't necessarily stay in close touch once the trouble passes. It is not during crisis, however, that we develop an appreciation for God's presence. Pure appreciation for His presence emerges from the daily walk, in the mundane more than the miraculous.

> Your Word is a lamp for my feet
> and a light on my path.
>
> *Psalm 119:105*

When we rub shoulders with Christ day-to-day, His wisdom and knowledge rub off on us little by little—wisdom being the application of knowledge, knowing what to do with what we know.

The psalm above paints such a beautiful word picture of this. His Word is "a lamp for my feet," guiding the steps I'm taking right now. His Word is also "a light on my path," a guide for my immediate future. God's Word sheds light on our present path and on our immediate future so we'll know what steps to take. But for further, future instruction, we must keep checking with Him every day.

May the Lord of peace Himself
give you peace always in every way.
2 Thessalonians 3:16

I can't overemphasize the importance of peace as a real and practical benefit of our covenant relationship with God. His peace should not be an infrequent surprise but the ongoing rule of our lives.

The apostle Paul, in the verse above, underscored the essential nature of peace. Did you notice how crucial he considered peace to be? "Always . . . in every way."

Peace can be possible in any situation, but we cannot produce it on demand. In fact, we can't produce it at all. It is a fruit of the Spirit. God's peace has already been given to us if we have received Christ.

> Bring My sons . . . and My daughters
> from the ends of the earth—everyone called
> by My name and created for My glory.
> *Isaiah 43:6–7*

God's glory doesn't just reflect Him. It is the way He makes Himself known or shows Himself mighty. He wants to reveal Himself to us. And each way He accomplishes this divine task is His glory. God's glory is how He shows us who He is.

Therefore, when the Scripture declares that we were created for God's glory, I believe this means He wants to make Himself recognizable *to* us and *through* us. He desires that He be recognizable in us in all that we do. Living a life that glorifies God is synonymous with living a life that reveals God.

> There is no fear in love;
> instead, perfect love drives out fear.
> *1 John 4:18*

Have you ever feared that someone would cease loving you? Not only have I feared it. I've experienced it! God has carefully and graciously allowed some of my fears to come true so I would discover that I would not disintegrate. God taught me to survive on His unfailing love. It wasn't fun, but it was transforming!

The one thing neither you nor I could survive is the loss of God's love, and that is a loss we will never have to try. His love endures forever. That's what is meant when the Scripture says that "perfect love drives out fear."

From eternity to eternity the Lord's
faithful love is toward those who fear Him.

Psalm 103:17

Few prisoners have people who are on the outside standing by them throughout lengthy incarcerations. Most people would just as soon forget prisoners existed. They are the unpeople of our society.

The same trend appears among Christians. The best of our churches tend to welcome those captive at first. But if that person doesn't "fix" pretty quickly, they will probably soon be despised.

In gracious contrast, God stands by us until we are free, never forsaking us. He is the only one who is not repelled by the depth and length of our needs.

For You, Lord, are kind and ready to forgive,
abundant in faithful love to all who call on You.
Psalm 86:5

Perhaps you are loved by someone who is not very demonstrative. Many people have difficulty showing affection, but remember that God is not one of us.

Innate in the nature of His love—both *chesed* (the Hebrew word for God's love) and *agape* (the Greek word for God's love) is the demonstration of affection.

Because God is love, He cannot keep from showing it, even if He sometimes opts to demonstrate it through discipline. He loves us through blessing, answered prayer, loving chastisement, constant care, intervention, and much more.

Know the Messiah's love that
surpasses knowledge, so you may
be filled with all the fullness of God.
Ephesians 3:19

When you received Christ, God's Spirit took up residence inside of you, with the desire to permeate every inch of your life and fill up every hollow place with the fullness of His love.

God has what you need. He alone has unfailing love, and He wants to flood your life with it. The fullness of God is not a one-time occurrence, like our salvation. To live victoriously every day of our lives, we must learn to pour out our hearts to God, confess sin daily so that nothing will hinder Him, acknowledge every hollow place, and invite Him to fill us fully!

February

Father, I desire those You have given Me
to be with Me where I am.
John 17:24

God's Word is full of proclamations of
His love for you. He inscribed His love in
His Word so you would never have to wait
for a phone call. You can hear God tell
you He loves you every single time you
open His Word. So when you're feeling
unlovely, soak yourself in the proclamations of God's unfailing love for you!

Truly, He thinks about you constantly.
I think heaven will be heaven because He
will be there, but *He* thinks it will be
heaven because *you* will be there. No
matter what time of night you roll over in
bed, you will catch God in the middle of a
thought about you.

> . . . taking every thought
> captive to the obedience of Christ.
> *2 Corinthians 10:5*

God's goal for our thought lives is that we learn to think with the mind of Christ. Rarely will God release us from captivating or controlling thoughts by suddenly dropping them from our minds. God rarely performs lobotomies. If we simply forgot the object of our stronghold, we might also forget to praise Him for His deliverance.

But before we can get controlling thoughts out of our minds, they must become Christ-centered thoughts while still in our minds. The richest testimonies come from people He has made whole and who still remember what it was like to be broken.

The Lord your God is the One who
goes with you to fight for you against
your enemies to give you victory.
Deuteronomy 20:4

We don't become victors by conquer-
ing the enemy. We become victors through
surrender to Christ. We don't become
victors by our independence from the
enemy. We become victors by our dependence on God.

The road to freedom is a paradox. To
experience victory and freedom, we need
to become captives. We need to develop
minds captive to Christ. In this life, we are
most free when our minds are most capti-
vated by Him. Victorious lives flow from
victorious thoughts. And thinking victorious thoughts comes from setting our focus
on a victorious God.

You will know the truth,
and the truth will set you free.
John 8:32

Our unwillingness to be truthful about our lack of satisfaction in the Christian life keeps us from asking the right questions: Why do I find the Christian life lacking? How can I be more satisfied? Because we aren't truthful inside the circle of believers, the enemy tempts us to look outside for godless answers.

So not only is *God's* truth an absolute necessity in our progress toward complete freedom, but *our* truthfulness is a necessity as well. Psalm 51:6 says God desires truth and integrity in our inner selves. A combination of these two vehicles—God's truth and our truthfulness—will drive us to our desired destination.

What a man desires is unfailing love.
Proverbs 19:22 (NIV)

The Word of God uncovers the answer to our greatest psychological, emotional need, and puts it into a capsule phrase for us: our need for "unfailing love."

Please don't miss this! *Every human being longs for unfailing love.* Lavish love. Focused love. Radical love. Love we can count on. The taxicab driver, the plumber, the stockbroker, the runway model, the actress, the streetwalker, the drug pusher, the schoolteacher, the computer programmer, the rocket scientist, the doctor, the lawyer, the president, and the custodian all yearn for the same thing: unfailing love.

Do you think I cannot call on My Father,
and He will provide me at once with
more than 12 legions of angels?
Matthew 26:53

Jesus obviously had the power to open
the earth and swallow His opposition, but
He didn't. I believe He restrained Himself
because He trusted the sovereignty of His
Father. In difficult times we, too, need to
trust God's sovereignty.

This means if He has allowed something difficult and shocking to happen to
one of His children, He plans to use it
mightily, if the child will let Him. God did
not cause Judas to be a thief and a betrayer,
but He did use the fraudulent disciple to
complete a very important work in the life
of Christ. Satan used Judas, but God ultimately took it over for His good work.

> He will teach us about His ways
> so we may walk in His paths.
> *Micah 4:2*

The better we know God, the more we trust Him. The more we trust Him, the more we sense His peace when the wintry winds blow against us . . . and the world offers us nothing to fight back with.

I was amused recently at the grocery store by the label on a lotion that claimed to be an effective stress reliever. I could hear a baby screaming in the next aisle. I had a brief impulse to offer the lotion to the poor mom pushing the cranky cargo, but I was afraid I might get a little stress reliever thrown back in my face. The world just can't seem to come up with a real, lasting solution to the strains of life.

Don't worry about anything, but in everything,
through prayer and petition with thanksgiving,
let your requests be made known to God.
Philippians 4:6

To experience the kind of peace that
covers all circumstances, the Bible challenges us to develop active, authentic
(what I like to call "meaty") prayer lives.
Prayer with real substance to it—original
thoughts flowing from a highly individual
heart, personal and intimate.

Often, we do everything but pray. We
want something more "substantial." Even
studying the Bible, going to church, talking to the pastor, or receiving counsel
seems more tangible than prayer. But it's
time to roll away the stone of prayerlessness. It's the most prohibitive obstacle on
the road to a believer's victory.

I will look favorably on this kind of person:
one who is humble, submissive in spirit,
and who trembles at My word.

Isaiah 66:2

Can you imagine being one whom
God esteems or respects, one on whom
He looks "favorably"? What a wonderful
thought! But to remove the pride that
distances us from full fellowship with
Him, we must view it as a bitter enemy
and view humility as a dear friend.

Often our society looks on biblical
humility as a sign of weakness. Nothing
could be further from the truth. Being
filled with pride is easy. It comes quite
naturally. Humility, on the other hand,
takes a supply of supernatural strength
that comes only from those who are strong
enough to admit weakness.

> Remain in Me, and I in you.
> *John 15:4*

Every river has an upland source and an ultimate mouth. Rivers depend on and are always connected to other bodies of water. Likewise, peace like a river flows from a continuous connection with the upland Source, Jesus Christ—a timely reminder that this life will ultimately spill out into a glorious eternal life.

The present life is not our destination. (Hallelujah!) We who know Christ move over rocks and sometimes cliffs, through narrow places and wide valleys to a heavenly destination. Until then, abiding in Christ is the key to staying deliberately connected with our upland Source.

No condemnation now exists
for those in Christ Jesus.
Romans 8:1

You may be wondering how a person
ever recognizes whether or not his or her
life is glorifying God. Please don't feel
dismayed if you ever ask yourself this! He
never sheds light on our weaknesses or
shortcomings for the sake of condemnation. Rather, He makes us aware of our
hindrances so He can set us free!

None of us consistently glorifies God
in everything we say and do, but we can
still experience genuine liberation in
Christ. He wants to do more through your
life than you've ever heard, seen, or imag-
ined. So as you make progress, be sure to
turn around and give Him the glory. That
is what glorifies Him!

What then are we to say about these things?
If God is for us, who is against us?
Romans 8:31

God has a right to complete authority. He is God, the Creator of the heavens and the earth, the supreme Author of all existence. He reigns over all, and in Him all things exist. He is Lord, the Master and Owner of all living creatures. He is the covenant Maker and Keeper. He is holy.

As Lord, He will never ask anything of us that is not right, good, and open to the light. He is perfect and undefiled. He is also our Redeemer, the One who bought us from sin's slave master so we could experience abundant life. He bought us to set us free!

Build it up, build it up, prepare the way,
remove every obstacle from My people's way.
Isaiah 57:14

In Isaiah's day, villages prepared weeks in advance for a visit by their king. Workmen cleared a path and built a road to provide the easiest access for the king's entourage. If the king did not find the path adequately prepared, he would bypass the village and withhold his blessing.

We need to accomplish this task. Yes, we face obstacles that need to be removed, but we have the approval and blessing of the matchless King in our favor. We don't have to wonder if He's willing and able to deliver us from the bonds that are withholding abundant life. The question is whether or not we're ready to cooperate and prepare the way for our Liberator.

Though the mountains move and the hills shake,
My love will not be removed from you.
Isaiah 54:10

The Word of God uses the phrase "unfailing love" thirty-two times, and not once is it attributed to humans. Every single use of the phrase refers to God and God alone. Although the love of others can be rich and meaningful, only God's love is unfailing.

He is not only the answer to a thousand needs but a thousand wants. He is our chief desire in all of life. Oh, God, awaken our souls to see—You are what we want, not just what we need. Yes, our life's protection, but also our heart's affection. Yes, our soul's salvation, but also our heart's exhilaration. Unfailing love—a love that will not let us go!

Jesus said to them,
"Do you believe that I can do this?"
Matthew 9:28

Sometimes God heals physical sick-
nesses, and sometimes He chooses greater
glory through illness. He can always heal
physical diseases, but He does not always
choose to bring healing on this earth.

Scripture is absolutely clear, however,
that God always wills the spiritual captive
to be free. God's will is for us to know
Him and believe Him, glorify Him, be
satisfied by Him, experience peace in Him,
and enjoy Him. For God to have utmost
cooperation from us on this freedom trail,
we must believe that He is ready, willing,
and completely able.

> If you will not listen, my innermost being will
> weep in secret because of your pride.
> *Jeremiah 13:17*

Beware of the fact that pride often disguises itself. I have known people, for example, who thought they were too far gone to save—too wicked, too sinful. Such people would be shocked to hear that even this attitude is a form of pride as well. They think their sin or problem is bigger than God.

Pride is a boulder in the road on our journey to freedom. The size of the boulder differs with each of us according to the degree to which we struggle with it. But to go forward from here, God must empower each of us to roll the boulder of pride off our road to liberty.

He feeds on ashes. His deceived mind has led
him astray, and he cannot deliver himself, or say,
"Isn't there a lie in my right hand?"
Isaiah 44:20

How many times have I fed on ashes
instead of feasting on the life-giving Word
of God? How many times has my deluded
heart misled me? How many times have I
tried to save myself?

I could fall on my face this moment
and praise God through all eternity for
finally awakening me to say, "This thing
in my right hand is a lie." I can remember
one thing in particular I held on to with a
virtual death grip.

Beloved, whatever we are gripping to
bring us satisfaction is a lie—unless it is
Christ. He is the Truth that sets us free.

The peace of God, which surpasses
every thought, will guard your hearts
and your minds in Christ Jesus.
Philippians 4:7

I decided to bring home the impact of this passage by paraphrasing it from a negative standpoint, turning this prescription for peace into a no-fail prescription for anxiety. My result looked like this:

"Do not be calm about anything, but in everything, by dwelling on it constantly and feeling picked on by God, with thoughts like, 'And this is the thanks I get,' present your aggravations to everyone you know but Him. And the acid in your stomach, which transcends all milk products, will cause you an ulcer, and the doctor bills will cause you a heart attack, and you will lose your mind."

One thing I do: forgetting what is behind and
reaching forward to what is ahead . . .
Philippians 3:13

I think many well-meaning Christians take out of context this exhortation about "forgetting what is behind," and apply it as a command from God and Scripture never to look at the past.

That's not what Paul was saying. He was talking about the trophies he had to leave behind to follow Christ. God's Word clearly expresses what a good and effective teacher the past can be.

The past will be a good teacher if we will approach it as a good student, from the perspective of what we can gain and how God can use it for His glory.

"You are My witnesses," declares the Lord, "that I am God. Yes, and from ancient days I am he."
Isaiah 43:12–13 (NIV)

When she was in second grade, my daughter Amanda illustrated a truth about the centrality of God. She was telling me something she had prayed over at school that day. I said, "Oh, Amanda, do you know how much it means to Mommy for you to make God a part of your day?"

I'll never forget her answer: "You're so silly, Mommy. You know God made the day. I'm just glad He made me a part of His."

I was stunned. She expressed through her childlike faith the meaning of God's wonderful name, the "Ancient of Days."

They are to teach what is good,
so that they may encourage the young
women to love their husbands and children.
Titus 2:3–4

If we live long enough, each of us will be barren. Are we to assume our fruitfulness has ended? Do we exist until death only on memories and large doses of fiber? Why, then, does barrenness come to all women around fifty years of age? Were we meant to sit around for the next thirty or forty years and twiddle our arthritic thumbs? God is far too practical for that!

When older women pour their lives into younger women and their children, they are birthing spiritual offspring. Older women are a necessity in the body of Christ. God calls us to be fruitful and multiply until He calls us home.

Look, I have inscribed you on the palms of My
hands; your walls are continually before Me.
Isaiah 49:16

I once heard a Christian child psychol-
ogist discuss the necessity of some conflict
and power struggle with teenagers. He
explained that a certain amount of difficulty must naturally arise as children
become young adults, or parents would
never be able to "help them" out of the
nest and on to independence. He said, "If
the bond we had with them as infants did
not change, we would never be able to let
them go."

All our lives, however, God retains the
strong feelings toward us that infants
evoke in their parents, because He never
has to let us go! He's not rearing us to
leave home, but to *come* home!

When a man dies, will he come back to life?
If so, I would wait all the days of my
struggle until my relief comes.
Job 14:14

Thank goodness, the loss of something or someone dear never has to mean the end of abundant, effective, or even joyful life for any Christian. These may seem to pause for a while as grief takes its course, but those who allow their broken hearts to be bound by Christ will experience them again. Our Savior is the God of resurrection life, no matter what kind of death has occurred to a believer.

When our hearts have been shattered by loss and sadness, we have an opportunity to welcome a supernatural power into our lives—the power to live again on this earth when we'd rather die.

Those He foreknew He also predestined to be
conformed to the image of His Son.

Romans 8:29

The life of a Christian is never about sameness. It's always about change. That's why we must learn to survive and once again thrive when change involves heart-breaking loss. We're being conformed to the image of Christ.

Whenever your heart is hemorrhaging with grief and loss, never forget that Christ binds and compresses them with a nail-scarred hand. Life will never be the same, but you have the invitation from Christ to rise to a new life—a more compassionate life, a wiser life, a more productive life. And yes, even a better life. Sound impossible? It is without Christ.

Now the Lord is the Spirit; and where the
Spirit of the Lord is, there is freedom.
2 Corinthians 3:17

I begin each day in God's Word. And somewhere in the midst of my morning time with God, I ask Him to satisfy all my longings and fill all my hollow places with His lavish, unfailing love. This frees me from craving the approval of others and requiring others to fill my "cup." Then, if someone takes the time to demonstrate love to me, that's the overflow. I'm free to appreciate and enjoy it, but I don't require it emotionally.

See how God's love brings freedom? Not only are we freed; we are able to free others from having to boost us up all the time. Where the Spirit of the Lord's lavish love is, there is freedom!

He knows the way I have taken; when He
has tested me, I will emerge as pure gold.

Job 23:10

No matter how long we have walked
with God, we will still have days that seem
dark. In those times God tells us to trust
in His name and rely on who He is.

So let the verse above be a blessing to
you when you don't know what to do.
When you feel you've lost your way, take
heart! He knows the way that you take.
Stand still, cry out, and bid Him come to
you! He will lead you on from there.

And when once again you see the light,
you'll be able to look back and notice the
footprints you made in the night. Never
will He hold your hand more tightly than
when He is leading you through the dark.

Keep Your servant from willful sins;
do not let them rule over me. Then I will be
innocent, and cleansed from blatant rebellion.
Psalm 19:13

Virtually anything that cheats you of
what God has for you could be considered
sin. I say this with compassion, but I must
say it, because we may not be recognizing
how Satan has taken advantage of normal,
healthy emotions. We easily view adultery,
robbery, or murder as sin, but we often
don't realize that sin can also be anything
we allow to grow between us and the
completing work of God.

So the first step in freedom is agreeing
with God's Word about your personal
stronghold or high place. The believer
who is still bowing down to the enemy in
her thought life cannot be fully liberated
from captivity.

The result of righteousness will be peace;
the effect of righteousness will be
quiet confidence forever.
Isaiah 32:17

Obedience to God's authority doesn't come easily for any of us. I heard one of the preachers I most admire say (quoting Nietzsche, oddly enough) that the life of the disciple requires a "long obedience in the same direction."

But are we saddled with nothing but sacrifices in this long obedience of ours? Hardly. Oh sure, obedience to God often entails not going our own way, not doing as we please. But if peace is the fruit of righteousness, then joy is the wine from the fruit! Joy will ultimately flow from obedience, and few things display God's splendor more appealingly!

Make Your way to the everlasting ruins, to all
that the enemy has destroyed in the sanctuary.

Psalm 74:3

You may have taken many looks back
at your life and found nothing but reasons
to be angrier or more depressed. I understand. I've done exactly the same. Then I
learned the difference between rebuilding
and preserving.

I was reminded of this as I stood at the
Acropolis in Athens. Our guide estimated
how much money they spend every year
"preserving the ruins." We do the same
thing ourselves. Rather than working with
God to rebuild, we just keep revisiting and
preserving. We never get over it. But that's
about the best we can do, unless we make
sure never to go back there without God,
our only sure Restorer.

March

There is no God like You . . . keeping the
gracious covenant with Your servants who
walk before You with their whole heart.

1 Kings 8:23

I have been to every extreme and back
with God. But if I had to define my relationship with Him in one single statement,
I would say He is the absolute joy of my
life. I don't just love Him. I love loving
Him. Surrendering my heart to Him has
not been a sacrifice. I don't know any
other way to say it: He works for me.

I am hesitant to say all of this because
I would be sickened to think I might sound
proud of my relationship with God. Please
hear my heart: the greatest joy of my life is
the very thing I deserve the least. It is an
absolute gift of grace. Yet it is one He will
gladly extend to anyone who offers Him
his or her whole heart.

The Lord is near the brokenhearted;
He saves those crushed in spirit.

Psalm 34:18

Can you remember when you lost your first tooth? Rode your first two-wheeler? Lived through your first day of junior high? These were monumental experiences, yet you may or may not even recall them. But if I asked about the first experience that shattered your heart, you'd likely remember everything—down to the last detail. Somehow having your heart broken is in a class all by itself.

But one of the primary reasons God sent His Son to earth was to bring tender salve and relief to those whose hearts have been broken. Binding up the broken-hearted is one of His greatest priorities.

> Who among you walks in darkness,
> and has no light? Let him trust in the name
> of the Lord; let him lean on his God.
> *Isaiah 50:10*

We cannot escape the warfare of the Christian life. Satan doesn't take time off for good behavior. Every day can bring trouble, but every day we have a blessed Troubleshooter.

Satan seeks to disgrace us, accuse us, and condemn us. We must daily set our faces like flint on the face of Christ and follow Him step by step to victory. Yes, you and I will still veer periodically from the path, no matter how obediently we want to walk. We are pilgrims with feet of clay. But no matter how long the detour has been, the return is only a shortcut away, because His light will always lead us right back to the path.

> How beautiful you are, my darling.
> How very beautiful! Behind your veil,
> your eyes are like doves.
> *Song of Songs 4:1*

The face of the bride was always veiled in the ancient Eastern world. The lifting of the veil from the face was one of the most intimate parts of the wedding night.

When Christ finally sees the lovely face of His bride, His beloved, He will not be disappointed. You will be a beautiful bride. The intimacy we will share with Him is beyond comprehension. We do not know what form it will take, but we will experience oneness with Him in complete holiness and purity. A knitting together of two spirits perhaps. Until then, bask in the assurance that Christ sees you as beautiful and desirable.

> We would not trust in ourselves,
> but in God who raises the dead.
> *2 Corinthians 1:9*

The level of trust we have for God is a monumental issue in the life of every believer. Many variables in our lives affect our willingness to trust God. A loss or betrayal can deeply mark our level of trust. A broken heart never mended can handicap us terribly when challenged to trust. Trusting an invisible God doesn't come naturally to any of us.

Our trust relationship with Him grows only when we step out in faith and make the choice to trust. The ability to believe God develops most often through pure experience. "I found Him faithful yesterday. He will not be unfaithful today."

The Spirit's law of life in Christ Jesus has
set you free from the law of sin and of death.

Romans 8:2

One of the most beautiful elements of
salvation is its simplicity. Christ has done
all the work on the cross already. Your
response includes four elements:

1) Acknowledge that you are a sinner
and cannot save yourself. 2) Acknowledge
that Jesus is the Son of God and only He
can save you. 3) Believe that His crucifix-
ion was for your personal sins and that
His death was on your behalf. 4) Give
Him your life and ask Him to be your
Savior and Lord.

Christ is the only entrance to the freedom trail. Be sure your relationship with
Him is up close and personal.

God wanted to make known to those among
the Gentiles the glorious wealth of this mystery,
which is Christ in you, the hope of glory.
Colossians 1:27

We have no hope whatsoever of God's being recognizable in us if the Spirit of Christ does not dwell in us. If we are not occupied by the Holy Spirit, we have nothing of God in us for Him to show. Christ is a human being's only "hope of glory."

We glorify God to the degree that we externalize the internal existence of the living Christ. A life that glorifies God is not something we suddenly attain. As we spend time in the presence of God, His glory both transforms us and radiates from us. As we grow in spiritual maturity, the Spirit of Christ becomes increasingly recognizable in us.

There is a generation that curses its father
and does not bless its mother.
Proverbs 30:11

As we consider any sins of our parents that we don't want to imitate or pass down, we should be careful not to curse them by demeaning and belittling them. A mere seven verses after God described generational sin to Israel in Exodus 20:5, He told them to honor their parents.

You can ask God to help you view any sins of your parents for the opportunity to avoid repeating them in your life or your children's. You can take a deeper inspection than ever before to learn and gain understanding. But you can be honest and still avoid belittling them as people. Such behavior is no option for believers.

Do you not know that if you offer
yourself to someone as obedient slaves,
you are slaves of that one you obey?
Romans 6:16

Until my mother's dying day, every
time I asserted myself about anything, she
reminded me of the time our family doctor
told me I couldn't go swimming because I
had an ear infection. Mom said I squinted
my eyes at him and said, "Oh yeah? Well,
you're not the boss of me!"

The problem is, God did not design us
to boss ourselves. He formed our psyches
to require authority so we'd live in the
safety of His careful rule. Satan tries to
draw us away from God's authority by
making us think we can do just fine as our
own producer and director. But we quickly
learn what miserable bosses we are.

Look at how great a love the Father has given us,
that we should be called God's children.
1 John 3:1

Why do we have such trouble believing and accepting the love of God, even though unbelief regarding His love is the ultimate slap in His face? The world came into being from the foundation of God's love. He nailed it down for us on the cross. Can you imagine the grief of our unbelief after all He's done?

You may say, "But I just can't make myself feel like God loves me." Belief is not a feeling, dear one. It's a choice. We may live many days when we don't feel loved or lovely, but we can choose to take God at His Word in spite of our feelings and emotions.

When pride comes, disgrace follows,
but with humility comes wisdom.
Proverbs 11:2

We have a crippling tendency to forget what God has done for us. For a while, we're humbled. Then, if we do not guard our hearts and minds, we begin to think we must have done something right for God to have been so good to us. Therein lies another road to captivity.

Several years ago, I began developing the habit of confessing and repenting of pride daily, even if I may not have been aware of its presence. I asked God to show me where it was raising its head or sneaking up on me. He so often shows me little bits of pride that, if left to grow, could be devastating. May each of us learn to guard ourselves against these lures to captivity.

And He did not do many miracles
there because of their unbelief.
Matthew 13:58

Five obstacles block our access to the
benefits God wants for us:

1) *Unbelief*—
which hinders us from knowing God.
2) *Pride*
which prevents us from glorifying God.
3) *Idolatry*
which makes us unsatisfied with God.
4) *Prayerlessness*
which blocks us from His peace.
5) *Legalism*
which stops our enjoyment of Him.

These hindrances keep us separated
from the birthright God intends for us.

It does not depend on human will and
effort, but on God who shows mercy.

Romans 9:16

Have you had a time when you were
surrendered to Christ in the midst of real
difficulty and you found His peace beyond
understanding? Can you also say, as I can,
that you have had an absence of peace in
much less trying circumstances? Have you
ever wondered what the difference was?

When we are in crisis and finally give
up trying to discover all the answers to the
whys in our lives, His unexpected peace
washes over us like a summer rain. But in
far less strenuous circumstances, we may
not be as desperate or as likely to turn
them over to God. Peace comes only in
situations that are completely surrendered
to the sovereign authority of Christ.

I will be with you when you pass through
the waters, and when you pass through the
rivers, they will not overwhelm you.
Isaiah 43:2

I doubt that any believer feels God's wonderful presence every second of every day. Sometimes we're challenged to believe He's with us simply because He promised. That's faith.

On some occasions, He may purposely alter the evidences of His presence to bring the most benefit from our experience. Sometimes we receive the most benefit from seeing *many* visible "prints" of His invisible hands during a difficult season. Other times we profit from seeing *fewer* evidences. God does not love us less during those seasons in life. He simply desires to grow us up and teach us to walk by faith.

> Everything is possible
> to the one who believes.
> *Mark 9:23*

When I talk about believing God, I don't mean just believing *in* God. I mean *believing* God, believing what He says.

We can believe in Christ for salvation in a matter of seconds and yet spend the rest of our days believing Him for little more. Eternity can be well secured while life on earth remains shaky at best.

We can believe *in* Christ, accepting the truth that He is the Son of God. We can believe *on* Christ, receiving eternal salvation. Yet there may still be times when we fail to stand firmly in our belief, choosing not to find Him trustworthy day to day.

Enter and possess the good land the
Lord your God swore to give your fathers.
Deuteronomy 6:18

A crucial reason exists for facing our generational strongholds head-on: unless we purposely seek them, they can remain almost unrecognizable, but they will not remain benign. Family ruins continue to be the seedbed for all sorts of destruction in our lives.

We tend to think of generational hand-me-down baggage as part of who we are rather than how we're bound. In many cases we grew up with these chains, so they feel completely natural. We're apt to consider them part of our personalities rather than a yoke squeezing abundant life out of us.

Christ has liberated us into freedom.
Therefore stand firm and don't submit
again to a yoke of slavery.
Galatians 5:1

Just as God's primary agenda for us is redemption, Satan's primary agenda is to blind people to the Redeemer. But once we are redeemed, our completion becomes God's primary agenda.

When God began stirring the message of *Breaking Free* within me, He gave me two statements to build on: 1) Christ came to set the captives free, and 2) Satan came to take the free captive. We are the free. Our liberty is a fact. But according to Galatians 5:1, we can still return to a yoke of bondage—only not if we cease cooperating with the enemy and start living in the reality of our liberty.

I will rebuild and not demolish you,
and I will plant and not uproot you.
Jeremiah 42:10

The only reason the sun rises every day is because God gives it His permission. He's never had a wink of sleep, and nothing is hidden from His sight. God has been God through every single day of your heritage.

If you're dealing with some ancient ruins, He was there when they crumbled. He knows every detail. He knows exactly how you've been affected, and His expertise is reconstruction. After all, Christ was a carpenter by trade. Nothing has ever been allowed to crumble in a Christian's life or heritage that God cannot reconstruct and use.

> They would not be like their fathers,
> a stubborn and rebellious generation,
> a generation whose heart was not loyal.
> *Psalm 78:8*

Between every unfaithful generation and every faithful generation is one person who is determined to change. And you could be that link. So could I.

Perhaps no one in your family was overtly sinful, but they were simply uninvolved in Christ's kingdom. Maybe you would like to be a link that takes your family line from an unfulfilling life of aimless religion to a passionate life of relationship with Christ. Perhaps your prayer for your grandchildren and your great-grandchildren might be a love for missions or a passion for ministry. Whatever it may be, you can be that link!

For God loved the world in this way:
He gave His One and Only Son.
John 3:16

God had only one arrow in His quiver. The most perfect arrow ever to exist—a masterpiece, priceless to Him. Cherished far above all the hosts of heaven. Nothing could compare. His only heritage. His only Son.

But as God looked on a lost world—desperate and needy and in the clutches of the enemy—His heart was overwhelmed. Though they had sinned miserably against Him and few sought Him, God had created them in love and could not love them less. So love reached sacrificially into the quiver and pulled forth the solitary arrow. Yes, God so loved the world.

> I will say to the Lord, "My refuge and
> my fortress, my God, in whom I trust."
> *Psalm 91:2*

Life's way of reacting to a crushed, broken heart is to wrap tough sinews of flesh around it and tempt us to promise we'll never let ourselves get hurt again.

But that's not God's way. Self-made fortresses not only keep love from going out; they keep love from coming in. And He knows we risk becoming captives in our own protective fortresses.

Only God can put the pieces of our heart back together again, close up all the wounds, and bind it with a porous bandage that protects the heart from infection but keeps it free to inhale and exhale love.

Come to Me, all of you who are weary
and burdened, and I will give you rest.
Matthew 11:28

Our souls can manifest physical symp-
toms of need. I like to think of it this way:
Just like my stomach growls when I'm
hungry for physical food, my spirit tends
to growl when I'm in need of spiritual
food. So when a checker at the grocery
store seems overtly irritable or grouchy, I
sometimes grin and think to myself, "I bet
her kids woke up before she had a chance
to have her quiet time!"

I can assure you that my personality is
distinctively different when I haven't had
the time I need with the Lord. My soul
can do some pretty fierce growling! How
about yours?

In Your presence is abundant joy;
in Your right hand are eternal pleasures.
Psalm 16:11

How realistic is the dream of living happily ever after? See for yourself:

In the parable of the talents, Jesus said (referring to Himself): "His master replied, 'Well done, good and faithful servant! You have been faithful with a few things; I will put you in charge of many things. Come and share your master's happiness!'" (Matt. 25:21, NIV).

There you have it. Jesus is happy. And He wants you to share His happiness—to live happily ever after. Until then, He gives us a sudden splash of happiness here and there so we can wet our toes in what we'll be swimming in for all of eternity!

You have turned things around,
as if the potter were the same as the clay.
Isaiah 29:16

Please allow God to engrave this truth on your heart: liberty and authority always go hand in hand.

During the ministry of the prophet Isaiah, captivity was imminent for the children of Israel because they had a serious authority problem. So he used the example of a marred piece of pottery to help them see this issue more clearly.

In essence, God was saying, "Let's get this straight: Me, God. You, human. Me, Creator. You, creature. Me, Potter. You, clay. You obey . . . not for My good but for yours."

Draw near to God,
and He will draw near to you.
James 4:8

God created us to be attached to Him, so He made us with a very real need *to be* attached. Therefore, people who detach themselves from truth inadvertently attach themselves to something else—to lies that defraud and extort.

In reality, there is no such thing as a completely independent human psyche. That's why to entice us, Satan offers us alternate attachments masquerading as fulfillments to our inner needs.

But any attachment other than God is a fraud. Wrong attachments mean we are growing in our dependence and reliance on something other than God.

Assuredly, I will set you free and care for you.
Assuredly, I will intercede for you.
Jeremiah 15:11

I grew up in a stronghold of fear. I longed to find a safe place to hide. I desperately wanted someone to take care of me. But from the realm of my own painful experience, let me alert you to a toxic emotional cocktail: a relationship made up of someone who has an unhealthy need to be taken care of, and someone who has an unhealthy need to caretake. This relationship will end up extorting God-given liberties and will prove fraudulent.

Any place we have to hide is not safe. In Christ, we find the freedom to be safely exposed! If only we could understand that God's authority does not imprison us. It sets us free!

In repentance and rest is your salvation,
in quietness and trust is your strength.
Isaiah 30:15 (NIV)

Have you ever experienced a season in your life when you knew what would rescue you, but you ran from it? Like me, you may rank these memories among your greatest regrets. Surely, everyone has run from real answers at one time or another.

But the same equation that first led us to Christ also applies to these situations: "In repentance and rest is your salvation!" Eternal salvation, of course, requires that we repent of our sins and depend on the work of Christ. Our need of deliverance, however, does not end once we become Christians. We still need lots of help avoiding snares and pitfalls. Let's receive it, not run from it.

The Lord is waiting to show you mercy,
and is rising up to show you compassion.
Isaiah 30:18

We can picture God being merciful and forgiving when we accidentally get ourselves into a mess, but we almost cannot imagine how God can be compassionate when we're outright rebellious.

Oh, what a disservice we do when we try to humanize God by imagining Him to be the best of humanity rather than being all-together God! Yes, His righteousness demands that He bring painful chastisement into our lives if we do not grab hold of His reaching hand and turn to Him wholeheartedly, but His loving compassion demands that He reach out to us even in our rebellion.

We have not received the spirit of the world,
but the Spirit who is from God, in order to know
what has been freely given to us by God.
1 Corinthians 2:12

The liberty of Christ was ours at the
moment we received Him as Savior. But if
this internal gift is not released externally
through obedience, we may never experience it.

When we receive Christ as Savior, we
receive His liberating Spirit, but we must
understand that the freedom never leaves
the bounds of His Spirit. Therefore, our
liberation is expressed as reality only in
the places of our lives where the free Spirit
of God is released.

We are free when, and only when, we
allow Him to be in control.

God proves His own love for us in that
while we were still sinners Christ died for us.
Romans 5:8

I have to admit, God's right to rule is
not my primary motivation for pursuing
the obedient life. I resist obeying someone
strictly on the basis of his or her position.
This will probably shock you, but I probably would have chanced eternity in hell
rather than bend my knee to any ruler just
because he was in charge.

So I cannot understand how such a
miracle of grace has come to me, but it
has. This may seem silly, but I love Him so
much that sometimes I can't wait for Him
to ask me to do something a little difficult,
because I want to obey Him. Trusting and
obeying Him is a constant reminder of a
perpetual miracle in my life.

I consider that the sufferings of this present
time are not worth comparing with the glory
that is going to be revealed to us.
Romans 8:18

Remember the wedding feast in Cana
of Galilee? The master of the banquet
made a statement about Jesus that always
touches my heart. It just describes Him so
well: "Everyone brings out the choice
wine first and then the cheaper wine after
the guests have had too much to drink;
but you have saved the best till now"
(John 2:10 NIV).

Jesus always seems to have something
greater waiting up around the bend. I
would never claim divine inspiration, but
Christ has proven Himself true so often, I
believe I can say with all confidence that
He has greater things just ahead for you.

April

It is the Lord your God who goes with you;
He will not leave you or forsake you.

Deuteronomy 31:6

One morning on my way to work, I pranced into my favorite little coffee shop and made my usual order: "a banana nut bagel with plain cream cheese, please." The server looked at me cheerfully and said, "We're not carrying that kind any more. Is there something else I can get you today?"

I stood there stunned, my eyebrows pinned like two barrettes to my hairline, until someone finally bumped me out of the way. As I walked to the car, I looked up and inquired, "Could I have one thing around this place that I can count on?" Yes. He will never leave us or forsake us.

> Give thanks to the Lord, for He is good.
> His love endures forever.
>
> *Psalm 136:1 (NIV)*

The thing that is of utmost importance to captives seeking complete freedom is this: God's works change, but His love stays steady and strong. The moment we think we've grasped His ways and figured out His methods, they will change.

Kings will rise and fall, but His love endures forever. Riches will come and go, but His love endures forever. Sometimes we'll be healed from physical afflictions and sometimes we won't, but His love endures forever. The heavens and earth will pass away . . .

But His love endures forever.

Many a man proclaims his own loyalty,
but who can find a trustworthy man?
Proverbs 20:6

This verse suggests something important about unfailing love. Paul described *agape* love as a supernatural love that only God fully possesses and only God can give. It's the New Testament word for God-love, just like *chesed* is the Old Testament word for God-love.

The only way we can love with *agape* is to pour everything else from our hearts and ask God to make them pitchers of His *agape*. Before we can even begin to give God-love away, we've got to fully accept it ourselves. To love others with anything close to God's love, we must be convinced that He loves us with perfect love.

> Let them give thanks to the Lord
> for His faithful love and His wonderful
> works for the human race.
> *Psalm 107:8*

God's unfailing love extends to the most rebellious captives and most afflicted fools. Psalm 107 is refreshingly clear: His love motivates wonderful deeds for the worst of men and women who cry out in their troubles.

The Hebrew word for "wonderful" is *pala*, meaning extraordinary, miraculous, marvelous, astonishing. These kinds of adjectives seem like they would be limited to God's *good* children, don't they? Yet His Word tells us He does extraordinary, miraculous, marvelous, astonishing things for the worst of the worst who cry out to Him . . . because He loves them.

Lord, You are my lamp;
the Lord illuminates my darkness.
2 Samuel 22:29

Our bulging prisons prove that rebellion can lead to literal incarceration. But it can just as easily lead to emotional cells of darkness and gloom. Although certainly not all depression is a result of rebellion, willfulness is definitely able to lead to it.

I think depression is especially likely if the rebel was formerly close to God. Now that I know the indescribable joy of intimacy with God, I know that living outside His fellowship would depress me.

So I am thankful God allows darkness to follow rebellion, because sometimes He uses darkness to lead us to the light!

We have put our hope in the living God.
1 Timothy 4:10

The worse possible thing that could result from our disobedience would be God giving up on us. Yet He continually strives with His captive children until they are free. Although God never excuses our sin and rebellion, He is fully aware of what drives our actions.

When I was growing up, I had no idea why I was making some of the poor decisions I was making. But God knew. Even though my rebellion was still sin, His heart was full of compassion. Through loving chastisement, He continued to strive with me, waiting patiently for me to leave my prison. No matter how long we struggle, God is not giving up on us.

Then the Lord became jealous
for His land and spared His people.
Joel 2:18

Even if we've drained all the human resources around us dry, God is our inexhaustible well of living water. He may allow the life of a captive to grow more and more difficult so that she will be more desperate to do what freedom in Christ requires—but He will never divorce her. He woos, and He waits.

The measures God takes to woo us to liberty may be excruciating at times, but they are often more powerful evidences of His unfailing love than all the obvious blessings we could expound. Few truly know the unfailing love of God like the captive set free.

We did not follow cleverly contrived myths
when we made known to you the power and
coming of our Lord Jesus Christ.
2 Peter 1:16

In the days before I began to enjoy the fullness of Christ, I somehow knew God's Word was true and that the problem rested with me. But for the life of me, I couldn't figure out what the problem was. I served Him. I even had a love for Him, however immature. But I still fought an emptiness that kept me looking for love and acceptance in all the wrong places.

Never once in my youth did I hear the clear teaching about the Spirit-filled life. Perhaps this is the reason I refuse to shut up about it now. Either Jesus Christ can satisfy us and meet our deepest needs, or God's Word is deceptive.

God is spirit, and those who worship
Him must worship in spirit and truth.
John 4:24

Don't get the idea that *spirit* implies
invisible. God definitely has a visible form,
however glorious and indescribable. But
we do not presently have eyes that can
behold the spirit world.

Yet just as surely as God is spirit, He is
also love. Love is not only something God
does; it is who God *is*. He would have to
stop *being* in order to stop loving.

Our temptation is to try humanizing
God because we are limited to understanding love as a verb. With God, however,
love is first and foremost a noun. It's what
and who He is.

I pray that you . . . may have power, together
with all the saints, to grasp how wide and long
and high and deep is the love of Christ.
Ephesians 3:18 (NIV)

We study so many other things, but
how about exerting some of our energy
into grasping the love of Christ? The word
for "grasp" in this verse means to lay hold
of, to seize with eagerness and sudden-
ness. I've experienced a few times when I
seemed to suddenly grab hold of the enor-
mity of Christ's love for a moment.

Can you think of a time when you
were suddenly awash with the magnitude
of His love for you personally? If not, ask
Him to make you more aware. God's love
is demonstrative. Ask Him to widen your
spiritual vision so you can behold unexpected evidences of His amazing love.

> We see that they were unable
> to enter because of unbelief.
>
> *Hebrews 3:19*

I believe the church is ill. She is pale and frail. Not because of judgment. Not because of neglect. Not because she doesn't have plenty to eat and drink. The meat of God's Word and the drink of His Spirit are there for the taking. Not because of warfare. She's bruised by the enemy, but he's not the one who is actually making her sick. He's just taking advantage of the opportunity.

No, her malady comes from within. Christ's bride is ill with unbelief. And the main reason why we don't recognize the illness is because most of us have suffered with it all our lives.

> He did not waver in unbelief at
> God's promise, but was strengthened
> in his faith and gave glory to God.
> *Romans 4:20*

Several years ago I slowly began noticing my energy level was lower than usual. After a blood test, the doctor called and immediately put me to bed for two weeks with a fierce case of mononucleosis. A few months later, I could not believe how good I felt. I had been sick for so long, I had forgotten how wellness felt.

The same thing happens with unbelief. When we've had the ailment so long, we don't remember how good authentic belief feels. The healthiest Christians you'll ever meet are not those with perfect physiques but those who take a daily dose of God's Word and choose to believe it works!

This is how we have come to know love:
He laid down His life for us.
1 John 3:16

You may say, "You don't know what I've been through." Please hear my heart. I am completely compassionate, because I've also been hurt by people who were supposed to love me. But let me say this: no matter how many people have made you feel unloved, the heavenly Father has done so much more to show you that you *are* loved.

If need be, make a list of ways you've become convinced no one could truly love you. Then make a corresponding list of ways the God of all creation has told you differently. I assure you that no list could compare to God's.

You will keep in perfect peace the mind that is
dependent on You, for it is trusting in You.
Isaiah 26:3

Freedom from strongholds is serious business. In-depth study and deliberate application of truth are not just helpful but are absolute necessities for those who choose liberty. We win freedom on the battlefield of the mind.

Notice in Isaiah 26:3 the inclusion of trust in the life of the one who possesses a steadfast mind. Only a trusting heart will approach God honestly with the secret struggles of the mind.

When we offer a trusting heart and an honest, open mind to God, we can be sure renewal is on its way.

> Listen! My love is approaching.
> *Song of Songs 2:8*

For several reasons, I am absolutely positive my husband, Keith, loves me. He shows me in all sorts of ways. For one thing, he tells me he thinks about me often during the day. I know this is true because he calls me at least once or twice at work every day. He testifies of his love for me to others. Often someone will tell me they've seen Keith, then they'll remark, "He sure seems to love his wife."

If you're married and your spouse is not as loving, please don't despair! I can tell you that God graciously delivered Keith and me from filing for divorce on several occasions. Don't give up! God can work miracles!

I fear that, as the serpent deceived Eve by his cunning, your minds may be corrupted from a complete and pure devotion to Christ.

2 Corinthians 11:3

Few biblical subjects are more controversial and debated than spiritual warfare and the battlefield of the mind. But many events and passages of Scripture demonstrate that Satan deals directly with the human mind.

In the parable of the soils, Jesus said Satan comes and takes away the Word sown in some people (Mark 4:15). In the story of Ananias and Sapphira, Peter said Satan had filled their hearts to lie to the Holy Spirit (Acts 5:3). In today's verse, Paul warned that Satan indeed seeks to lead believers' minds astray. Clearly, Satan engages us in our thought lives.

The weapons of our warfare are not
fleshly, but are powerful through God
for the demolition of strongholds.
2 Corinthians 10:4

The word *demolish* implies a kind of
destruction requiring tremendous power—
divine power, to be exact. I believe much
of the reason why believers have remained
in a yoke of slavery is because we swat at
our strongholds like they are mosquitoes.

Strongholds, however, are like concrete
fortresses we've constructed around our
lives block by block, ordinarily over the
course of years. We created them (whether
or not we were aware) for protection and
comfort. But these fortresses inevitably
become prisons. At some point we realize
we no longer control them. Rather, they
control us.

Those who make them are just like them,
as are all who trust in them.
Psalm 135:18

Satan's goal is to be worshiped. This is what he has always wanted. This is what fuels his rebellion against God.

But if Satan can't get people to worship him directly, he accomplishes his goal by tempting people to worship something or someone other than God.

God created us to worship. Each of us will worship something. The focus of our worship can be determined by the gaze of our eyes—by what or who is the object of our primary focus. And believe me when I tell you: whatever we worship, we will also obey.

You should no longer walk as the Gentiles
walk, in the futility of their thoughts.
Ephesians 4:17

Imagine how being the victim of rape
could captivate your mind and nearly
destroy you. Deep compassion floods my
heart as I realize that perhaps even you
know this from personal experience. The
loss of a loved one, too, can be a devastating experience. And if we don't surrender
our minds to Christ, it can take us from
appropriate grief and mourning to a life-
time of agonizing captivity.

Remember, Satan fights dirty. He will
jump on anything that could keep you
from centering your thoughts on Christ.
But the more you know God's Word, the
quicker you will recognize his attempts.

She went down to the spring,
filled her jug, and came up.
Genesis 24:16

The empty places in our lives become the playground of the enemy. Imagine, for example, a golf course. The flags tell the golfer where the holes are. I believe something similar happens to us in the unseen. None of us have reached adulthood without some holes in our lives, and you can be sure the enemy has flagged every hole as a target.

We spend untold energies in anger and bitterness over why those holes exist and who is to blame. But healing begins when we recognize how vulnerable those empty places make us, tally the cost of filling them with useless things, and seek our wholeness in Christ alone.

He awakens Me each morning; He awakens
My ear to listen like those being instructed.
Isaiah 50:4

I believe with all my heart, based on
this wonderful verse, that though we can
hear from God at any time, He awakens
us in the morning with a supernatural
capacity to hear from Him. At the beginning of the day, we haven't gone the wrong
way yet.

Every day, God wants to sustain someone who is weary. Sometimes I'm that
person. Sometimes you are. But God
always has a word to speak to us if we
will not be rebellious and draw back. He
always offers us the daily treasure of a
fresh morning word.

If you forgive people their wrongdoing,
your heavenly Father will forgive you as well.
Matthew 6:14

When I finally bent the knee to the Prince of Peace over hurts in my childhood, I realized He was directing me to forgive the person who hurt me. God did not insist on my forgiving for the sake of that person but for peace in my life. When at last I allowed Him to govern everything concerning my past, not only did the Prince give me His peace, He actually brought good from something horrible and unfair.

He will do the same for you, as well. Once you begin to surrender to Him, even in your most painful area, He will give you a supernatural ability to forgive.

In all their suffering, He suffered,
and the Angel of His Presence saved them.
Isaiah 63:9

I believe Christ still grieves when He sees hearts in unnecessary turmoil. He desperately wants His people to experience His peace. When we allow the Prince of Peace to govern our lives, peace either immediately or ultimately results. Peace accompanies authority.

You may not ever *feel* like giving your circumstance, loss, or hurt over to Him, but you can *choose* to submit to His authority out of belief and obedience rather than emotion. Obedience is always the mark of authentic surrender to God's authority.

I am the Lord God, who teaches
you for your benefit, who leads you
in the way you should go.
Isaiah 48:17

We hopefully will be able to discover a few reasons why we are so reluctant to submit to God's authority, but we must remember that bending the knee is ultimately a matter of pure obedience.

As I said, I finally had to turn some of the hurts of my childhood over to God's sovereign authority because I realized they would consume me like a cancer. If you have not yet bowed the knee to God's authority over areas of your past, something is holding you captive. You can have the peace of Christ no matter what your circumstances, but you must believe, bend the knee, and learn to receive.

Consider what I say, for the Lord will
give you understanding in everything.
2 Timothy 2:7

I think a writer should never appear
desperate for the reader to care about her
work. It just isn't seemly. She should just
do her best, and place the result out there.
I do believe that. But in this case, I just
can't do it. The contents of these pages are
so important to me, I desperately want
them to be important to you.

I hope that this book will pull on your
life so powerfully as we continue together
through the year that the bondage of
mediocre discipleship will never again be
acceptable. Christ calls us to a place of
breaking free. He woos us to the place of
absolute freedom—the only kind of freedom that is real.

I was like a docile lamb led to slaughter. I didn't
know that they had devised plots against me.
Jeremiah 11:19

I shake my head and marvel that I
once thought the only people captive were
the spiritually lost. God pried open my
comfortably closed mind in the most effective way: from the inside out.

If anyone had told me that Christians
could be in bondage, I would have argued
with all the volume a person can muster
when a yoke of slavery is strangling her
neck. I was the worst kind of captive: a
prisoner unaware, the kind of prisoner
most vulnerable to her captors, the easiest
prey there is. A Christian is held captive
by anything that hinders the abundant
and effective Spirit-filled life God planned
for him or her.

> So Israel became poverty-stricken because of
> Midian, and the Israelites cried out to the Lord.
> *Judges 6:6*

The people of God have little defense against the destructive nature of the enemy without the power of God working in their favor. In this scene from the Book of Judges, the Israelites had prepared shelters for themselves for protection against their enemy. But the Midianites came in like a swarm of locusts, impossible to count. They invaded the land and ravaged it.

We can be saved and yet continually live in defeat because the enemy can outwit us if we do not depend on the Holy Spirit and the Word of God. We've got to know that we're being swarmed, wise up to the Word, learn what our rights are, and use the equipment God has given us.

God said to me, "You are not to build
a house for My name because you are
a man of war and have shed blood."
1 Chronicles 28:3

I believe God willingly tells His children why they are being oppressed if they
are willing to listen.

Of course, we would rather God just
fix our messes. We don't want to get into
the reasons why. "Lord, just set me free! I
don't want to know why I got into this
shape. Let's not dig up all of those old
bones from the past. Just set me free and
let's get on with life."

But God says, "I want you to know
what went wrong so that the next time
you're in this same situation, you'll make
different choices; you'll seek Me instead."

Who can come down against us?
Who can enter our hiding places?
Jeremiah 21:13

Often when we're oppressed, instead of cooperating with God and going with Him to a place of freedom, we go into isolation and hide. We hide behind our jobs. We hide behind the busy things we do at church. We hide behind activity—the captivity of activity.

But God will sometimes allow things to get bad enough that we will be forced to come out of hiding and look up. He does not allow us to be oppressed so that we will be defeated, but so that we will ultimately be victorious. Victory always begins with a cry for help. When we come to the end of ourselves and do what liberty demands, amazing things start to happen.

Save Your people, bless Your possession,
shepherd them, and carry them forever.
Psalm 28:9

O God, as we move into a new month of *Breaking Free,* we invite You to do a work in us that we cannot even explain. We dedicate this journey entirely to You and give You every bit of glory.

We pray, Lord, that we will not raise up a hand to hinder or stop You, because sometimes the truth does hurt. We know You desire to have the fullness of our lives so You can cause us to live in victory.

So we humble ourselves before You, and we ask You to do a mighty work in our hearts so we can proclaim Your name the rest of our lives. You alone are God. There is no other Savior.

May

The Lord gave them rest on every side
according to all He had sworn to their fathers.
Joshua 21:44

Strong's dictionary gives a definition
for the Hebrew word *nachath* (meaning,
rest) that tickles me. It says the word
means "lighting down."

I can picture my grandmother with a
fly swatter in her hand and a serious look
on her face. "Whatcha doin', Nanny?" I'd
ask. "I'm waiting for that filthy fly to light
down somewhere so I can smack it."

Somehow, we often believe we are like
that fly. We think if we light down for a
second, God's going to whack us. Untrue.
We are not flies. God's desire is for us to
rest in Him, to light down on His truth
and be set on who He is.

Look to Abraham your father,
and to Sarah who gave birth to you in pain.
Isaiah 51:2

We know from Galatians 3:29 that we are "Abraham's seed, heirs according the to the promise." And by looking back at what God did through Abraham's life, we discover that we can . . .

1) Believe God for the impossible.

2) Admit the futility of taking matters into our own hands.

3) Believe God still loves us even we take a temporary detour—if we agree to return to His path.

4) Believe God can still call us righteous based on our faith in Him, even if our righteous acts are like filthy rags.

5) Believe that God's ultimate blessing follows our obedience.

If we walk in the light as He Himself is in the light, we have fellowship with one another.
1 John 1:7

Imagine going to heaven, where God lovingly shows you His plan for your life. It begins with the day you are born. And once you received Christ as Savior, every day that follows is outlined in red.

On many of those days, two sets of footprints appear. You inquire: "Father, are those my footprints every day, and is the second set of prints when You joined me?"

He answers, "No, My precious child. The consistent footprints are Mine, going toward the destiny I planned for you, hoping you'd follow. The second set of footprints are when you joined Me."

Happy are the people whose strength is in You,
whose hearts are set on pilgrimage.

Psalm 84:5

The Bible frequently tells us that we should walk God's way instead of ours. But remember that walking consistently doesn't mean walking perfectly. It means we may stumble, but we will not fall!

How often do we remind ourselves, in the daily-ness of our walk with God, that we are on a journey leading to a glorious heavenly city? He wants to guide us every day in His own wisdom and knowledge. Remember, He's the One with the plan!

Yes, life may take us from trial to trial, but because we are walking with God, we can be sure He is taking us "from strength to strength" (Ps. 84:7).

Keep yourself in the love of God, expecting the
mercy of our Lord Jesus Christ for eternal life.
Jude 21

I remember trying a little experiment once as I spoke to a group of women on the subject of God's love. I asked each of them to look eye-to-eye with the person beside them and say, "God loves me so much."

Almost instinctively, they turned to one another and said, "God loves *you* so much." I stopped them, brought the switch in words to their attention, and asked why they were struggling with my request.

See, we readily accept God's love for others, but we struggle with the belief that He loves us equally, radically, completely, and unfailingly.

The grace of the Lord Jesus Christ,
and the love of God, and the fellowship
of the Holy Spirit be with all of you.
2 Corinthians 13:13

I used to struggle with God's love for me because I knew my own sins and weaknesses—all the reasons He shouldn't love me. Surely everyone else wasn't the mess deep inside that I was! (Of course, some people can be so full of self-righteousness, they seem convinced God loves them best of all.)

But why do we have such difficulty believing God could love with the same unfailing love those we perceive as good and those we perceive as bad? It's because we relentlessly insist on trying to humanize God. We tend to love people according to how they act, and we keep trying to create God in our image.

With You I can attack a barrier,
and with my God I can leap over a wall.
Psalm 18:29

While tracing the travels of the apostle Paul through Greece and Rome, I once stood on the grounds of ancient Corinth facing the ruins of a once thriving city. I remember asking the guide to identify the fortress I could see in the distance, positioned on the tallest mountain. She said, "It's an ancient stronghold. Virtually every ancient Greek city had a stronghold or fortress on top of its highest peak. In times of war, this place was considered practically impenetrable and unapproachable."

Yes, strongholds are imposing. I could see why opposing armies gave up. Sadly, we have often done the same thing. My prayer is that we will say, "No more!"

People will live there, and never
again will there be a curse of destruction.
So Jerusalem will dwell in security.
Zechariah 14:11

As you think about a stronghold that you've experienced, what part did insecurity play in it?

Without a doubt, insecurity played a major role in the strongholds the enemy built into my life. An important part of learning to live in victory has come from discerning the heart rumblings of insecurity. I have learned to dramatically increase my prayer life and time in God's Word when my security is threatened.

I haven't always responded rightly in times of insecurity, but when I have, Satan has failed to gain an advantage.

When he tells a lie, he speaks from his own
nature, because he is a liar and the father of liars.

John 8:44

Picture the captivity of your thought
life like a prison cell wallpapered in lies.
Demolition of strongholds really begins
when we expose and tear down the lies
that fuel them in the first place. We cannot
repeat this fact enough: *deception is the
glue that holds strongholds together*. By
the time a stronghold exists, our minds
are covered in lies.

Where do these lies originate? According to Jesus' words in John 8:43–45, Satan
himself is the "father" of lies. But he uses
them only because he is a totally defeated
foe. Lies are all he has. That's why he has
to be so adept at using them.

Be transformed by the renewing of your mind,
so that you may discern what is the good,
pleasing, and perfect will of God.
Romans 12:2

Satan became far more sophisticated in my adult life. One yoke he put around my neck involved someone who came to me for help. Satan twisted the truth to make me believe I was responsible for this person. The Holy Spirit signaled me not to get involved, but I chose what I thought was religious duty over obedience. It was a trap set by the enemy.

This person was certainly worth helping, but I was not the one to help. Her problem was out of my league. I learned in this situation that if you don't listen to God and obey in the early stages, the less discernment and strength you have.

> Then they may come to their senses
> and escape the Devil's trap, having been
> captured by him to do his will.
> *2 Timothy 2:26*

We can think of Satan's subtleties as his camouflage. Generational yokes often go undetected because they blend in so well with our personalities. We excuse some of these yokes as simply being the way we are. We might even say, "My mother was like this, and so was hers!" Or, "My grandfather raised my father not to take a handout from anyone."

Maybe you are beginning to see a well-camouflaged chain you've inherited. You don't have to decide, "Well, I'm stuck with it, so I may as well be proud of it." In Christ we are not stuck with anything but Him. Praise His name!

Please forgive your brothers' transgression
and their sin—the wrong they caused you.
Genesis 50:17

The enemy specializes in taking advantage of any refusal to forgive. I'll describe an all-too-common scenario. A family has a feud over the family business. The grown siblings cease speaking to one another and do not allow their children to associate. They harbor bad feelings so long that those who refused to forgive become unforgiving people. They have little in common except that most of them are mad at someone all the time.

Perhaps alienation like this has been your family's way of life for so long that it doesn't even seem strange! Let's be brave enough to see if we are perpetuating division and unforgiveness in the family line.

> "As I live"—this is the declaration
> of the Lord God—"you will no longer
> use this proverb in Israel."
>
> *Ezekiel 18:3*

Do your children ever accuse you of being unfair about something? Every once in a while, mine did—and it hurt! Then just in case I didn't get the point, they'd go on and on with the subject until I was weary of hearing it.

At those times I might have said words like these: "I've heard this out of your mouth more times than I ever wanted to! What you're accusing me of isn't even true! Now let that be the end of it!"

God was saying something like that in Ezekiel 18, which He went on to explain and illustrate. But we can summarize it in two words: *personal responsibility.*

No, in all these things we are more than
victorious through Him who loved us.
Romans 8:37

We must believe the truth over the
enemy's lies. We can be freed from the
effects and practices of the sins in our
lineage. Allow me to say gently and with
much compassion: you are not the exception, and neither is your situation. In all
things we can be overcomers but, indeed,
only through Him who loves us.

We've talked before about belief versus
unbelief. Down in the deepest part of our
hearts, do we look at old habits and snares
or at our parents and say, "It's no use; I
will always be this way"? Please turn from
any unbelief, or it will keep liberty from
ever becoming a reality in your life.

> Their arm did not bring them victory—
> but by Your right hand, Your arm,
> and the light of Your face.
>
> *Psalm 44:3*

Most people I know who live free today have experienced a serious stronghold or hindrance they fought to overcome. They usually appreciate and apply victory more readily because they've experienced the misery of defeat firsthand. I rarely meet people who have come to trust God fully who haven't also painfully confronted the fact that they can't trust themselves.

If you stick with God, you will become so unique in the body of Christ that whether or not you ever wanted to be a leader or example to others, you will be. That's just what happens when people become victors.

This is what love for God is:
to keep His commands. Now His
commands are not a burden.
1 John 5:3

Rebellion begins with fun and games, but eventually it leads to hard work. God allows rebellion to become a heavy burden after a while. Certainly not all physical affliction is caused by rebellion, but rebellion can definitely result in it. I can think of a time in college when I rebelled against God. I lost my appetite and became physically ill. I know I wasn't the first one in history to become sin-sick.

Yes, even though all of God's responses toward us are evidence of His love rather than His wrathful condemnation, He loves us enough to make us ultimately miserable in our rebellion.

He was like one people turned away from;
He was despised, and we didn't value Him.
Isaiah 53:3

Betrayal is motivated by selfishness but not always evil. I don't believe every spouse who has an extramarital affair means to devastate the betrayed husband or wife. Indeed, a betrayer may be sincerely regretful of the pain selfishness caused.

In Jesus' case, though, Judas's betrayal took the worst of forms. Even though Christ knew Judas would betray Him, I believe He was still devastated by it.

Heart-shattering betrayal is one of the hardest experiences we ever encounter. To know how best to bind up the heart it breaks, Christ chose to experience it.

My goal is to know Him and the power of His resurrection and the fellowship of His sufferings.
Philippians 3:10

The Lord doesn't often tell us why He allows wounds to come to us, but He did graciously give me this Scripture to explain one reason why I experienced a painful betrayal. I pray continually to be Christlike, but whenever He lets me "fellowship" with Him in a few of His sufferings, I tend to whine and carry on.

Few of us will escape betrayal in one way or another, but will we choose to fellowship with Christ in the midst of it? Will we choose to trust the sovereignty of our heavenly Father who allowed it? Betrayal can either hurt and hurt. Or hurt and help. The choice is up to us.

We who live are always given over to death
because of Jesus, so that Jesus' life may
also be revealed in our mortal flesh.
2 Corinthians 4:11

A while back, God introduced a season
of loss into my life that spanned the most
difficult two-year period of my adulthood
to date. We lost our son, Michael, to his
birth mother after having him for seven
years. My mother was diagnosed with
cancer and died. Two of my best friends
moved away, as did our oldest daughter,
Amanda, who left for college.

Life involves change. Change involves
loss. Loss involves death of one kind or
another. But every time we suffer loss, we
encounter an opportunity for the loss to
bring gain for Jesus' sake by allowing His
life to be revealed in us.

Many of the Jews who came to Mary
and saw what He did believed in Him.
John 11:45

Christ never allows the hearts of His
own to be shattered without excellent
reasons and eternal purposes. Jesus dearly
loved Mary and Martha, yet He purposely
allowed them to suffer a loss. Our Father
will never allow our hearts to break for
trivial reasons.

We may never see the reasons the same
way Mary and Martha did, but could we
walk by faith and believe the best of
Christ? You see, the most debilitating loss
for a Christian is not the loss of a loved
one but the loss of faith. Do you see how
the loss of faith could turn into a form of
bondage?

The marriage of the Lamb has come,
and His wife has prepared herself.
Revelation 19:7

This verse and those that surround it in Revelation 19 describe the corporate gathering of all believers and Christ at the marriage supper of the Lamb. But this verse in particular implies an important responsibility of the bride.

Notice in the second line the qualifier of the bride's actions. She has "prepared herself." She has made herself ready. Past tense. We cannot make ourselves ready the moment we see Christ, any more than a woman can be prepared to meet her groom at the altar with three minutes' notice. I want to be ready, don't you? I certainly don't want to be caught with spiritual curlers in my hair!

Bow down to him, for he is your lord.
Psalm 45:11

An important part of making ourselves spiritually ready is studying and knowing our Groom, which is something we can learn a lot about from Psalm 45:

1) We can't help but love Him, for He loves us, gripped by our "beauty" (v. 11).

2) We can't help but respect Him for His character. "Grace flows from His lips" (v. 2).

3) We stand in complete awe of Him as He rides "triumphantly" (v. 4).

4) We experience complete joy in Him, more than all other "companions" (v. 7).

Behold your Groom—the One you're preparing for. Make yourself ready!

Who are you—
anyone who talks back to God?
Romans 9:20

From all appearances, my adorable youngest daughter came into the world to take over. By the time she was two years old, she liked to walk ahead of the rest of us so she could appear to have come by herself. She was born authoritative and seemed to assume that she, Keith, and I were all three on the same level. If I had a dime for every time I said, "Me, parent! You, child!" she would inherit a fortune!

Over and over again, God sets out in His Word that He is in control. He desires to change us from the inside out—renewing our minds, starving our self-destructive tendencies, and teaching us to form new habits by respecting His authority.

You say . . . "We will ride on fast horses"—
but those who pursue you will be faster.
Isaiah 30:16

Without God's intervention in our lives, we all tend to be pigheaded. We want to boss ourselves, but let's face it: bossing ourselves is a ticket to slavery. We need to consider carefully the impending disaster that awaits those who bear the marks of a rebellious child—one who:

1) Doesn't act like a child of God.
2) Isn't willing to listen to instruction.
3) Prefers illusions over truth.
4) Relies on oppression.
5) Learns to depend on deceit.
6) Runs from real answers.

Clay that insists on acting like the Potter will inevitably end up in pieces.

This is how we know that we remain in Him
and He in us: He has given to us from His Spirit.
1 John 4:13

In the form of the Holy Spirit, God
takes up residence in the lives of all who
receive His Son as Savior. God can no
more cease being love than He can cease
being spirit. Therefore, when the Spirit of
God moves into our lives, the love of God
comes, too.

See how it all fits together? Wherever
God is welcomed, His Spirit is loosed.
Wherever the Spirit is loosed, so is His
love. And wherever you find His loving
Spirit, you find freedom. And how is the
Spirit of God loosed? Through confessing
or agreeing with His Word. Every place
we allow the love of God to penetrate us,
we will be satisfied and liberated.

May they be made completely one,
so the world may know You have sent Me and
have loved them as You have loved Me.
John 17:23

This may absolutely amaze you, but did you know that God testifies to others how much He loves you? That's what Jesus was saying to His Father in this prayer from John 17.

Does this happen to be a new thought to you? Look how much God loves you. Christ wants the whole "world" to know that the Father loves you and me just as much as He loves His Son. God is so proud to love you!

Believer, let's get on our way to genuinely believing lives. Let's rise up from our sickbed of unbelief. Let's believe the love the Father has for us.

> Therefore, be imitators of God,
> as dearly loved children.
> *Ephesians 5:1*

God calls us to act like the dearly loved children we are. Take some time to give this admonition some thought. To gain insight, let's draw a parallel between God's children and the children of earthly parents. We don't need a degree in childhood development to imagine how differently children feel and behave based on whether or not they believe they are truly loved.

Sometimes, earthly parents are unloving or perhaps are unable to express love appropriately. God, though, is not human. He loves perfectly. Those who believe that God loves them will differ from all others, in both their attitudes and their actions.

God's love was revealed among us in this way: God sent His One and Only Son into the world so that we might live through Him.

1 John 4:9

God's love is unfailing, so any time we perceive He does not love us, our perceptions are wrong. But when we realize we've been believing a lie, our bonds lose their grip.

At those times we might pray something like: "I may not feel loved or lovable, but Your Word says You love me so much that You gave Your Son for me. I don't know why I continue to feel unloved, but at this moment I choose to believe the truth of Your Word. I rebuke the enemy's attempts to make me doubt Your love. And I also pray for forgiveness for the sin of unbelief."

I keep the Lord in mind always. Because
He is at my right hand, I will not be shaken.
Psalm 16:8

The Hebrew term for "mind" is *yetser*.
It sounds like what my siblings and I were
expected to say every time our dad, the
Army major, told us to do something. The
mind is certainly where we decide if we're
going to say "yes, sir" or "no, sir" every
time our heavenly Father gives us an
instruction or command.

One of the meanings of *yetser* is the
idea of a "frame," like a picture frame.
Our minds work to frame every circumstance, temptation, and experience we
have. We see events from our own perspective and context. So by winning the battle
over your thought life, how could that
help you "frame" situations differently?

Lord, You will establish peace for us,
for You have also done all our work for us.
Isaiah 26:12

One time when I had been hurt by someone close to me, the pain in my heart felt like a searing hot iron. During the day, I would read or quote Scripture when my thoughts began to defeat me, but my worst attacks came at night.

At the risk of being labeled a lunatic, I'll tell you what I did: when I got into bed at night, I turned to Scripture that spoke truth to my circumstances, and I would literally lay my head on my open Bible until I fell asleep. The Holy Spirit never failed to bring my mind comfort and relief—not because of the ritual, but because I believed by faith that He would accomplish what my posture symbolized.

So God heard their groaning,
and He remembered His covenant
with Abraham, Isaac, and Jacob.
Exodus 2:24

Just about every time you see God described in Scripture as remembering something or someone, He moves to act in their behalf. "He remembered," and therefore He came down to rescue them.

How does this apply to us? God knows our suffering from the very first pang. He desires, however, to hear us cry out to Him specifically for His help.

God never misses a single groan or cry of His children. He always has a rescue mission planned. When the time is right, you can be sure God will move in behalf of His children.

June

> We are not obligated to the flesh
> to live according to the flesh.
> *Romans 8:12*

Not all captivating thoughts come from painful experiences. Our thoughts can be held captive to someone or something that builds up our egos or satisfies our fleshly appetites. Simply put, captivating thoughts are controlling thoughts, things you find yourself meditating on far too often.

Taking thoughts captive to Christ does not mean we never have the thought again. It means we learn to "think the thought" as it relates to Christ and who we are in Him. When we relate our thoughts to Christ, they cause us less and less despair. They will not control us. With the power of the Holy Spirit, we will control *them*.

I will certainly bring health and healing
to it and will indeed heal them.
Jeremiah 33:6

Nothing could be more natural than a mother grieving the loss of a child. If ten years later, however, the mother is still completely consumed with the loss and bitterness that have eclipsed all comfort and healing, she has wedged a stronghold between appropriate grief and gradual restoration.

The enemy will capitalize on normal emotions of love or loss to swell them out of healthy proportion. They can consume our lives if we're not aware of his schemes. No, grieving is never sin. But disallowing God to minister comfort and healing to you over the passage of time is.

Who has known the Lord's mind, that he may
instruct Him? But we have the mind of Christ.
1 Corinthians 2:16

We possess the mind of Christ, but we
still have the full capacity to think with
the mind of the flesh. We are mentally
bilingual, you might say. But in order to
experience liberation in Him, we must let
His language become our native tongue.

Look at it this way: my older daughter
is almost fluent in Spanish, but she still
thinks mostly in English. Why? Because
she practices it more. Her thoughts follow
the language she uses most often.

The same concept is true of you and
me. We will think with the mental language
we practice most: ours or Christ's.

I see a different law in the parts of my body,
waging war against the law of my mind.
Romans 7:23

God will not release us from anything
that has enslaved us until we've come to
the mind of Christ in the matter.

Take the bondage of unforgiveness,
for example. When we want to be free
from the burden of not forgiving, we want
God simply to take that person out of our
minds. We want Him to wave a magic
wand so we'll never have to think about
that person again.

That's not how God works. He wants
to transform and renew our minds so we
can think the thoughts of Christ about the
person we are supposed to forgive.

*You are being renewed
in the spirit of your minds.*
Ephesians 4:23

In my travels, staggering numbers of women confess being involved in affairs. Often I am relieved to hear them say that they have repented and walked away in obedience to God. Just as often, however, they will say, "He's out of my life, but I can't seem to get him out of my mind."

I can see the sincerity in their hearts. God has forgiven the sin, but the mental stronghold is still overwhelming. I know it takes perseverance to see this through, but many people give up before the old thoughts give out! Promise to give God your complete cooperation. Take time to renew your mind. You will be victorious, and Satan will be defeated.

> Here is the endurance
> and the faith of the saints.
> *Revelation 13:10*

How does a believer get her thoughts to bow to the truth? By believing, speaking, and applying truth as a lifestyle. This step is something we live, not just something we do.

We can't just shout, "Sit!" and expect the dog to stay there for a week. We've worked a long time to get that dog to sit, but it's still not going to sit forever. We don't achieve victory once and never have to bother with that thought problem again. Our thought life is something we'll be working on the rest of our lives in our desire to be godly.

There is certainly no righteous man on
the earth who does good and never sins.
Ecclesiastes 7:20

Many situations or conditions in life
can keep us from truly enjoying God's
presence. Not spending adequate time
with Him, for instance, will greatly affect
our pure enjoyment of Him. Having an
underdeveloped prayer life will also rob
us of our joy, as can harboring bitterness
or anger at another person.

But the man or woman who studies
God's Word in depth yet still experiences
a consistent lack of enjoyment of God
often suffers from a condition with an
ugly name—*legalism*. We cannot please
God or find freedom in mere rule-keeping.
Never have. Never will.

Is it lawful on the Sabbath to do good
or to do evil, to save life or to destroy it?
Luke 6:9

The Pharisees had a superficial understanding of God and no enjoyment of His
presence. They never seemed to get the
idea that the Sabbath was something God
established for our benefit, not for our
imprisonment.

In the biblical account from Luke 6
where Jesus healed the man with the shriv-
eled hand, the greatest benefit Christ could
bring to him was a relationship with the
Savior. He chose to initiate that relationship through healing. But the Pharisees
tried to squeeze all the enjoyment out of
this event by replacing relationship with
regulations. We don't have to wonder who
enjoyed Christ more that day!

He has reconciled you by His physical body
through His death, to present you holy,
faultless, and blameless before Him.
Colossians 1:22

We each have a concoction of good,
bad, and ugly in our family lines. And we
need to make sure we didn't inherit any
hand-me-down chains that interfere with
the priceless benefits of our covenant relationship with Christ.

He broke the chains of all kinds of
bondage when He gave His life for us on
the cross. Many of us, however, still carry
them in our hands or have them dangling
from our necks out of pure habit, lack of
awareness, or lack of biblical knowledge.
We don't need to engage in family bashing
of any kind, but we do need to recognize
any generational bonds and ask God to
remove them.

I will make peace flow to her like a river,
and the wealth of nations like a flood.

Isaiah 66:12

God's Word does not say we'll have peace like a pond. If we were honest, we might admit to thinking of peaceful people as boring, like they're a breath from death. We are apt to think, "I'd rather forego peace and have an exciting life!" But when was the last time you saw white-water rapids? Few bodies of water are more exciting than rivers!

When God used the analogy of a river, He described a peace that can be retained while life twists and turns and rolls over boulders. It means to have security and tranquility while meeting many bumps and unexpected turns on life's journey.

My lips will glorify You because
Your faithful love is better than life.
Psalm 63:3

We can assume that our soul is hungry
and thirsty for God if we haven't partaken
of any spiritual food and drink in a long
while. Souls accustomed to soul food are
more likely to have a highly developed
appetite. In Psalm 63, David revealed that
he was accustomed to beholding the power
and glory of God. Therefore, he missed
God's refreshment when he didn't have it.

We have the same tendency. The more
we've been satisfied by God's love and His
presence, the more we yearn for it. On the
other hand, we can spend so much time
away from the Lord that we no longer feel
hungry or thirsty anymore. Only God can
satisfy our yearning souls.

Then you will delight yourself in the Lord, and
I will make you ride over the heights of the land.
Isaiah 58:14

God doesn't take our spiritual temperature under our tongue by the words we
say, nor in our ear by the impressive teach-
ings we hear, nor under our arm by the
service we perform. God takes our spiritual temperature straight from the heart.

See, the journey toward breaking free
is about a relationship, not regulations.
It's about learning to thoroughly enjoy
God's presence. Sometimes along the way,
your eyes will be opened to things you'd
rather not see. But when someone asks
whether or not you enjoyed this book, I
want you to be able to say with all your
heart, "Actually, I enjoyed God."

Because of the Lord's faithful love,
we do not perish, for His mercies never end.
Lamentations 3:22

When I refer to something we may have inherited, I mean anything we may have learned environmentally, anything to which we may be genetically predisposed, or any binding influence passed down through other means. I don't come to you on the basis of science or psychology but on behalf of the freedom Christ has come to offer you.

It's possible you may have inherited so much bondage that you can hardly stand looking back. My special prayer for you is that God will help you see some positives. I experienced some very ugly things in my childhood, but I can also see the merciful hand of God. Can you?

The boundary lines have fallen for me in pleasant
places; indeed, I have a beautiful inheritance.
Psalm 16:6

We don't have to disinherit or dishonor
our physical lineage to fully accept and
abide in our spiritual lineage. God fully
recognizes and desires to use both "lines"
to His glory, but our spiritual lineage can
overpower and disable any continuing
negative effects of our physical lineage.

Do not let the enemy get to you with a
spirit of heaviness. We are going to stand
on a positive approach even to our negatives, because bringing them before God is
the first step to healing and gaining freedom. If you encounter anything painful,
thank God immediately that He is ready
and willing to diffuse all things in your
heritage that are binding you.

Woe to the world because of offenses.
For offenses must come, but woe to that
man by whom the offense comes.
Matthew 18:7

Christ healed people in many different ways. Sometimes He did it through touch. Sometimes He did it through speech. In this passage from Matthew 18, Christ offered healing through truth.

I found significant healing in my study of this particular Scripture. I learned how important I was to Jesus as a child. I was also able to accept how much He despised what had happened to me.

And in perhaps the greatest lesson of all, I learned that Scripture is the strongest bandage God uses to bind hearts that were broken in childhood.

Take delight in the Lord,
and He will give you your heart's desires.
Psalm 37:4

Hearts entirely surrendered to God can ordinarily be trusted. For example, if a man or woman's heart belongs entirely to God and they do not long to be married or have children, they are probably called to singleness or childlessness to pursue other purposes for God. Psalm 37:4 could be translated to support this statement.

On the other hand, hearts that are *not* surrendered to God can seldom be trusted. Until we surrender our hopes and dreams to Christ, we really have very little way of knowing what would fulfill us.

> The foreign resident among you
> will rise higher and higher above you,
> while you sink lower and lower.
>
> *Deuteronomy 28:43*

A young Christian girl has a harsh, abusive father. She grows up with a fear and distaste for men. Satan supplies a slightly older woman who seems tender and caring. This comforting relationship turns into a physical relationship, so the young woman assumes she must be homosexual. In her heart she knows what she is doing is wrong, but she feels helpless without her new comforter. Soon she drops all relationships except those that support her fraudulent attachment to lies.

Scary, isn't it? But I use this obvious scenario to make my point that Satan will use our unhealthy attachments to keep us walking in our chains.

You did not abandon them in the wilderness
because of Your great compassion.
Nehemiah 9:19

When you begin to study the faithful, lifesaving, compassionate love of God in Scripture, you discover that the word often used for "compassion" is the Hebrew word *racham*, meaning "to soothe; to cherish; to love deeply like parents; to be compassionate and tender." (And now for my favorite part of the definition.) "Small babies evoke this feeling."

I have never experienced a more overwhelming, inexpressible feeling than the one my two little infants birthed in me. My babies brought out a capacity to love I had never experienced before. To think that our Father loves us like that. Wow!

Whoever drinks from the water that I will give
him will never get thirsty again—ever!
John 4:14

Christ's encounter with the woman at
the well introduces us to some realities of
life we desperately need to remember:

1) Our insatiable need or craving for
too much of anything is symptomatic of
unmet needs or "empty places."

2) Salvation does not equal satisfaction. You can be genuinely saved and still
be unsatisfied.

3) Satisfaction comes only when every
empty place is filled with the fullness of
Christ.

4) While salvation comes to us as a
gift from God, we find satisfaction in Him
as we deliberately surrender all parts of
our lives to Him.

He lets it loose beneath the entire sky;
His lightning to the ends of the earth.

Job 37:3

One night when all I felt like doing was sobbing, I decided to throw on the headphones and go for a walk. The night was pitch black. No one appeared to be out but me. But the more the music rang through my soul, the more the tears of my wounds turned to tears of worship. Finally, I stopped walking, lifted both my hands in praise, and worshiped Him.

Flashes of distant lightning began to burst like fireworks on the Fourth of July. And the more I sang, the more the Spirit of God seemed to dance to each streak of light. I haven't had many experiences like this, but it was like getting a sudden, flashing grasp of God's amazing love.

He has torn us, and He will heal us; He has
wounded us, and He will bind up our wounds.
Hosea 6:1

How can we characterize the difference between an aching heart and a broken
heart? The Bible defines a broken heart as
one that is hemorrhaging. Compressing a
hemorrhaging heart is the idea of applying pressure to a badly bleeding wound.
What a wonderful picture of Christ! A
crushing hurt comes, and the sympathiz-
ing, scarred hand of Christ presses the
wound. Just for a moment, the pain seems
to intensify, but finally the bleeding stops.

Are you beginning to see the intimate
activity of Christ when we're devastated?
And to think, this is the same One we
accuse of not caring when the crushing
moment comes.

> Why do you take Him to court for
> not answering anything a person asks?
> *Job 33:13*

Let me tell you how I deal with the "whys" of life—the ones to which I can't find the answers. I find as many answers as I can in God's Word, fill in those blanks, and then trust Him with the rest.

Sounds simple, but it's not. It's something I practice by faith every single day of my life, and I find great solace and rest in this method. Just knowing that God's good can come from life's bad is one of the most liberating concepts in the entire Word of God.

I know of no better way to say it. Until the rest of my blanks are filled in, the ones He has answered are enough for me.

I said, "I will confess my transgressions to the
Lord," and You took away the guilt of my sin.
Psalm 32:5

Each of us who has been victimized in
childhood can testify that the tendencies
toward certain sins dramatically increase
as a result. As part of my healing, I was
forced to take responsibility for my own
sins, whether or not another person's
actions escorted me toward them.

Perhaps you're like I was at one time.
You don't want to take responsibility for
your sins because you don't think they're
your fault. You may wonder, "How else
would I have responded after my reference point was so distorted?" But you see,
I don't think confessing sin is primarily
about fault. It's about freedom!

I am the resurrection and the life. The one
who believes in Me, even if he dies, will live.
John 11:25

Any kind of "death" is an invitation
to resurrection life for the believer. Nothing is more natural than grief after a
devastating loss, but those of us in Christ
can experience satisfying life again.

Perhaps the most profound miracle of
all is living through something we thought
would kill us. And not just living, but
living abundantly and effectively—raised
from living death to a new life. Yes, it's a
life that is indeed absent of something or
someone dear to you, but it is filled with
the presence of the Resurrection and the
Life. Will you continue to sit in a dark
tomb, or will you walk into the light of
resurrection life?

Tamar put ashes on her head and tore the long-
sleeved garment she was wearing. She put her
hand on her head and went away weeping.
2 Samuel 13:19

In the Old Testament, people covered
their heads with ashes as a symbol of
mourning. Ashes were a reminder of man's
mortality. Those who covered themselves
in ashes symbolically stated that without
God, they would be nothing more than
ashes.

Perhaps the reason I have a favorable
view of some of these ancient practices is
because I am so demonstrative, but I can't
help believing that we can all find a little
freedom in expression at times. Squelch-
ing emotions only stores them in explosive
containers. God's Word constantly recognizes our emotional side.

My eager expectation and hope is that . . .
Christ will be highly honored in my body.
Philippians 1:20

Have you ever noticed that you can experience freedom in one part of your life yet remain in bondage in another? Sometimes we allow God to have full authority in one area while refusing Him somewhere else.

How, then, can we be fully liberated? Can we study God's Word enough until we finally experience freedom? Can we pray ourselves into it? Can we rebuke the enemy so thoroughly that we shake loose from his grip? No. Until we choose to withhold no part of our lives from God's authority, we will not experience full freedom. The answer to liberty is giving Him everything.

For I have come down from heaven, not to do
My will, but the will of Him who sent Me.
John 6:38

Do you know what Christ's ultimate
purpose was during His earthly life? He
proclaimed it continually. The only begot-
ten Son came to do the will of His Father.

Yes, even the Father and the Son had a
Potter/clay relationship. Christ obeyed the
Potter. As an earthen vessel, Jesus had to
trust His Father's will completely. Though
rejection, suffering, and shame were part
of His experience, Christ accepted His
God-given ministry at every difficult turn
because He trusted His Father's heart.
"My food," He said, "is to do the will of
Him who sent Me and to finish His work"
(John 4:34).

> If we confess our sins, He is faithful
> and righteous to forgive us our sins and to
> cleanse us from all unrighteousness.
> *1 John 1:9*

Allow me to stress again that obedient lives are not perfect lives. Obedience does not mean sinlessness but confession and repentance *when* we sin. Obedience is not arriving at a perpetual state of godliness, but perpetually following hard after God.

Obedience does not mean living miserably by a strict, confining set of laws, but inviting the Spirit of God to flow freely through us. Obedience means learning to love and treasure God's Word and see it as our safety. Obedience is the crucial key that ignites the liberty of Christ and makes it a reality in life.

> The Lord is the stronghold of my life—
> of whom should I be afraid?
> *Psalm 27:1*

I have a nightmare—having to obey an unrighteous authority. In case you think obedience comes easy for me, let me clear up a few things. Submission and subservience are as easy to me as cuddling a litter of baby porcupines. A child who has been forced into things she didn't want to do usually grows up never wanting to be told what to do again—by anyone!

But the Lord has helped me learn how to handle this. I've slowly come to trust His sovereignty enough to believe that anyone I must obey on this earth had better be careful with me, or they will have God to answer to!

I, therefore, the prisoner of the Lord, urge you
to walk worthy of the calling you have received.
Ephesians 4:1

A profound change occurred in my
daily approach to God when I realized
God wanted me to walk with Him. For
years I asked God to walk with *me*. Talk
about the clay trying to spin the Potter! I
wanted to take my feet of clay and walk
where my heart led, counting on Him to
bless my sweet-if-selfish heart.

Finally I realized God's blessing would
come only when I did what He said. For
safety and the pure enjoyment of God, we
are so wise to learn to walk with God
instead of begging Him to walk with us.
Walking with God in pursuit of daily
obedience is the sure means of fulfilling
each of His wonderful plans.

July

> As my life was fading away,
> I remembered the Lord. My prayer
> came to You, to Your holy temple.
> *Jonah 2:7*

Many of us have expended unknown energy trying hard to topple these strongholds of ours on our own. We've tried pure determination, secular psychology, denial. But they just won't fall, will they? That's because they must be demolished.

And so God has handed us two sticks of dynamite with which to demolish our strongholds: His Word and prayer. What is more powerful than two sticks of dynamite placed in separate locations? Two strapped together. When we unite the power of the Word with the power of prayer, we ignite them with faith in what God says He can do.

A better hope is introduced,
through which we draw near to God.
Hebrews 7:19

Prayer keeps us in constant communion with God, which is the goal of our entire believing lives. Without a doubt, prayerless lives are powerless lives, and prayerful lives are powerful lives.

But believe it or not, the ultimate goal God has for us is not power but personal intimacy with Him. Yes, He wants to bring us healing, but more than anything, He wants us to know our Healer. Yes, He wants to gives us resurrection life, but more than that, He wants us to know the Resurrection and the Life.

> Therefore, Your servant has found
> the courage to pray this prayer to You.
> *2 Samuel 7:27*

Please let this truth sink in: It is never the will of God for warfare to become our focus. The fastest way to lose our balance in warfare is to rebuke the devil more than we relate to God.

The primary strength we have in warfare is godliness, which is achieved only through intimacy with God. Therefore, God will undoubtedly enforce prayer as one of the weapons of our warfare, because His chief objective is to keep us connected entirely to Him.

Prayer is not the means to an end. In so many ways, it is the end itself.

> Pursue righteousness, faith, love,
> and peace, along with those who call
> on the Lord from a pure heart.
> *2 Timothy 2:22*

The Bible does indeed speak specifically to the battles we face. It has much to say about fighting the good fight of faith and becoming well-trained soldiers. But throughout its sixty-six books, it has far *more* to say about the pure pursuit of God, of His righteousness, and of His plan for our lives.

So while we should give much time and thought to becoming well-equipped victors in the battles that rage against us, we should give *more* time to the pursuit of the heart of God and all things concerning Him. Much about warfare. More about God Himself.

Listen, my sons, to a father's discipline,
and pay attention so that you
may gain understanding.
Proverbs 4:1

When I first began to research the biblical history of God's people, I kept running into a conspicuous common denominator: idolatry.

I don't know why it was such a news flash. God warned His people over and over that if they did not resist the false gods of the nations, they would be snared and He would ultimately allow them to be taken captive. They didn't, and He did.

One sobering thing to keep in mind about the faithfulness of God is that He keeps His promises, even when they are promises of judgment and discipline.

For you did not receive a spirit of slavery to fall back into fear, but you received the Spirit of adoption, by whom we cry out, "Abba, Father!"
Romans 8:15

You and I as believers in Christ have been chosen to know, believe, and understand that God is God. Heaven is His throne. Earth is His footstool. Awesome creatures never cease day or night singing, "Holy, Holy, Holy, Lord God Almighty."

Lightning flashes from His throne. The winds do His bidding. The clouds are His chariot. The earth trembles at the sound of His voice. When He stands to His feet, His enemies are scattered.

And yet this very One is our Father, our Abba. He demands and deserves our respect. Without it, we are powerless.

I am the way, the truth, and the life. No one
comes to the Father except through Me.
John 14:6

Believing God is rarely more challeng-
ing than during those times when we have
strongholds that need demolishing. We've
battled most of these strongholds for years
and tried countless remedies in an effort
to be free . . . with very little success.

The enemy taunts us with whispers
like, "You'll never be free. You've tried a
hundred times, but you keep going back.
You're hopeless. You're weak. You're a
failure. You don't have what it takes."

But every one of these statements
about you is a lie if you are a believer in
Christ. You *do* have what it takes. You
have Jesus—the Way, the Truth, the Life.

Since we have the same spirit of faith in accordance with what is written, "I believed, therefore I spoke," we also believe, and therefore speak.

2 Corinthians 4:13

If you believe in Jesus Christ, you have been given this "same spirit of faith." The original word for "spirit" is literally translated "breath." When you speak God's Word out loud with confidence in Him—rather than having confidence in your own ability to believe—you are *breathing* faith. Believing and speaking the Word of God are like receiving blessed CPR from the Holy Spirit.

So please remember: it is always God's will for you to be free from strongholds. We may not be sure God wills to heal us physically, but He always wills to free us from the strongholds that bind us. Keep praying!

The Lord made David
victorious wherever he went.
2 Samuel 8:6

We can go along for quite some time thinking we've gotten our act together. We can live successfully for years . . . but not live victoriously. Oh, how wise we are to understand the mammoth difference!

Successfully describes how we handle the relatively manageable challenges that the unbeliever could manage just as well. Living "successfully" can simply mean that we've been spared some of life's most overwhelming problems. But *victoriously* describes how we live as overcomers in the midst of Goliath opposition. Living "victoriously" is our privilege and calling as redeemed children of God, no matter what life throws at us.

There are shouts of joy and victory
in the tents of the righteous.

Psalm 118:15

As much as I wish my testimony could be *defeat followed by salvation followed by complete victory,* it is not. My testimony actually goes something like this:

Salvation, confusion, misery, defeat, success, more defeat, unmitigated failure, then victory!

In essence, my testimony is that there is life after failure—abundant, effective, Spirit-filled life—for those who are willing to repent hard and work hard. Wholeness will only come when we give ourselves wholly to God and let Him fill every empty place in our lives.

I will never boast about anything except the cross
of our Lord . . . through whom the world has
been crucified to me, and I to the world.
Galatians 6:14

Yes, God can still use us, but we must
fall on our faces in desperation, taking full
responsibility for our own sin (no one
else's), receive His loving discipline, and
walk radically in the revealed truth of
God's Word.

Without exception, every one of the
overcomers I know personally who have
come back to their feet after terrible defeat
have lived in victory only through a radical walk with Jesus Christ in truth. For
folks like me, there's not a lot of gray. I
learned the hard way what can happen
when you wander too close to a hole. You
can fall in.

False messiahs and false prophets will arise
and perform great signs and wonders to
lead astray, if possible, even the elect.
Matthew 24:24

Tragically, Satan has duped the vast majority of our churches into imbalance regarding all things concerning or threatening him. Our human natures are drawn like magnets to polar points, and we unfortunately apply our fleshly extremes to our pulpits. We tend to give the devil far too much credit or not nearly enough.

I cannot say this strongly enough: it is imperative in these days to walk in truth and soundness of doctrine. We must not be taken captive in this hour of increased deception and wickedness. We must stay in the Word and claim Christ's victory over the enemy!

If we say, "We have fellowship with Him,"
and walk in darkness, we are lying and
are not practicing the truth.
1 John 1:6

While believers debate whether or not Christians can experience depression, our ranks are enduring it in record numbers. Obviously, we *can* and *have*. The verse above has been wrongly interpreted to mean that true believers do not experience seasons of darkness.

Believers are most assuredly people of light, but sometimes the darkness around us can be so oppressive, we can feel it. No, we are not "of" the darkness, but we can sometimes "feel" the darkness. The most wonderful insight offered by 1 John 1:6 is that our willingness to fellowship with God in the midst of our difficulty will usher forth rays of His wonderful light.

I called to the Lord in my distress, and I cried to
my God for help. From His temple He heard my
voice, and my cry to Him reached His ears.

Psalm 18:6

Take heart! Men and women of the
faith far more godly and effective than we
are (or ever will be) have battled depression. Remember, the defeat is not in
fighting depression, but in giving in.

Beloved, God never misses a single
tear of the oppressed. He sees our suffering and knows the depth of our need. He
anguishes, yet He waits . . . until the tears
that have fallen on dry ground or upon
the shoulders of others who are equally
frail are poured instead before His throne.
He waits—not until the oppressed cry out,
but until we cry out to Him. Only then
will we know the One and Only who
redeems us.

I know the plans I have for you . . .
plans for your welfare, not for disaster,
to give you a future and a hope.
Jeremiah 29:11

We often see ourselves as having such fragile, breakable souls. We live in fear of that which we are certain and convinced we cannot survive.

But as children of God, we are only as fragile as our unwillingness to turn and hide our face in Him. Our pride alone is fragile. Once its shell is broken and our hearts are laid bare, we can then begin to sense the caress of God's tender care.

Please know that God has a plan for you—a plan to give you "a future and a hope." And until His plan is revealed and realized, He will hold you just the same.

Whoever keeps His word,
truly in him the love of God is perfected.
1 John 2:5

We are to come and know the love of God by experience. His is a depth of love that surpasses any kind of limited knowledge our minds can now grasp. But we come to know it by trial as we walk with Him every day.

So we need to continually fan the flame of His love by reading Scripture, listening to edifying music, and praying often. We also need to avoid things in our daily routine that quench His Spirit. When we make a daily practice of inviting His love to fill our hollow places and make sure we are not hindering the process, God begins to satisfy us more than our favorite meal.

> We have come to know and to
> believe the love that God has for us.
> *1 John 4:16*

I continue to see this statement in my
mail: "I have such trouble really believing
and accepting how much God loves me."
So I began to ask God, "Lord, why?"

I offered Him several multiple-choice
answers to my own question: "Is it our
backgrounds? Our childhood hurts? The
unsound teaching we've received? Is it the
unloving people who surround us?"

I would have gone on, but He had the
gall to interrupt me without choosing even
one of my multiple-choice answers. As
clearly as a bell, the Spirit spoke to my
heart, "The answer to your question is the
sin of unbelief."

You will lead the people You have redeemed
with Your faithful love. You will guide them to
Your holy dwelling with Your strength.

Exodus 15:13

The child of God who trusts God's
love possesses security in His leadership.
God promises us that we are not left to
wander around aimlessly until we enter
heaven. He knows the plans He has for
us. He leads those whom He has redeemed
so that we will fulfill His wonderful plan.
What a comfort to know that the places
God chooses to lead us will always flow
out of His unfailing love.

Truly, God will never stop loving. We
can pour out frustration from our hearts
with total courage, because we know the
Father will never reject us or deprive us of
the security of our salvation.

Search me, God, and know my heart;
test me and know my concerns.
Psalm 139:23

Satan is extremely cunning. Therefore, our knowledge alone will never be enough to keep us protected. What you and I need is a watchman sitting guard on the walls of our mind. Here's the good news: we have One who is willing and able—One who knows us completely and is thereby the perfect candidate to guard our minds.

Giving Him watchcare over our mind is serious business, because surrendering our thought lives to Him is not just a means to more consistent victory. It's the safeguard against being given over to a depraved mind. We can persist so long in our willful, wrong thinking that God can give us over to our desires.

Watch yourselves so that you don't lose
what we have worked for, but you
may receive a full reward.
2 John 8

Don't become discouraged if you're a
person who wants to have a steadfast
mind in Christ but can't seem to gain
control of your thoughts. Welcome to the
club! We've all been there!

Just keep telling God how much you
want to give Him your whole heart and
mind. The wayward, defeated mind and
the willfully depraved mind are not the
same thing. Left unchecked, however, the
former can lead to the latter.

So try not to become weary in taking
your thoughts captive to make them obey
Christ. This is a desire He loves to honor.

I led them with cords of
human kindness, with ties of love.
Hosea 11:4 (NIV)

As I reflect on my personal history
with God and how He has been single-
handedly responsible for my liberty, I am
almost moved to tears over this verse.

We know from experience and from
our own study of Scripture that Satan, the
ultimate counterfeiter, also desires to lead
us . . . to our deaths. He presses the yoke
on our neck as he leads us with cords of
falsehood, lies, and deception.

But as you read on in Hosea 11:4, you
see that unlike the enemy, God's purpose
is to be "like one who eases the yoke from
their jaws; I bent down to give them food."
He leads us that He might save us.

What fruit was produced then from
the things you are now ashamed of?
Romans 6:21

Have you noticed that there is no such thing as a small act of disobedience? To disregard God's commands is a sure way to bear bitter fruit, sooner or later. Some of Israel's kings who otherwise followed God's ways still failed to tear down the high places of pagan worship. Ultimately, this oversight took its toll. A kingdom resulted in which God's own people sacrificed their children to pagan gods.

Truly, anything we exalt over God in our thoughts—even a little thing—is an idol, which is a terrible affront to God. It is also an open invitation to disaster. Never forget the ever-increasing nature of sin.

Your enemies will cringe before you,
and you will tread on their backs.
Deuteronomy 33:29

If you are aware of a stronghold that presently exists in your life, have you come to a place of agreeing with God's Word and confessing all sin involved?

If you are aware of a stronghold in your life that you've never agreed with God about and confessed all sin involved, would you be willing to do so now?

If you are not aware of any stronghold in your life, can you remember a time in the past when Christ led you to freedom through honesty and confession? The divine power of God is available to all of us who will agree to apply it.

At once something like scales fell
from his eyes, and he regained his sight.
Acts 9:18

Imagine you have agreed with God about the stronghold and confessed the sin involved. God then begins to open your eyes to the lies plastered like graffiti on the walls of your mind. Lies like, "All men will hurt you." "I am worthless." "You can't say no." (I could go on and on with the lies I've believed.)

I want to say something with tenderness and much compassion: if you know a stronghold exists in your life but you can't identify the lies, you are still a captive. If you've not recognized the lies that are keeping you glued to your prison cell, ask God to drop the scales from your eyes and help you see!

Test me, Lord, and try me;
examine my heart and mind.

Psalm 26:2

We will not be free until we adopt the
mind of Christ in any matter that has
enslaved us. If a believer has allowed Satan
to build a stronghold through an adulter-
ous relationship and she finally repents
and desires to be free, her mind will not be
released until she has torn down the lies
and reprogrammed with the truth.

She would probably beg God simply
to remove the person from her mind. But
God knows that little would be accom-
plished by doing that, and she would be
vulnerable to a similar attack. Rather than
drop the person from her mind, He wants
her to think the thoughts of Christ toward
the situation and the person.

The one who sows to his flesh will reap
corruption from the flesh, but the one who sows
to the Spirit will reap eternal life from the Spirit.

Galatians 6:8

If someone has repented of an ungodly
relationship and has walked away from it,
the first thing she must do is tear down the
lies and put up the truth. She must begin
to meditate on truth that speaks to her
specific challenge. She needs to fill her
mind with things that feed the Spirit and
avoid situations that feed the flesh.

Starving the flesh and feeding the Spirit
is the process by which people or things
that are out of God's will for us will finally
depart from our thoughts. Over time, the
person who was formerly filling our
thoughts will fill them less and less until,
finally, the thoughts are neglected and
starved to death.

Love the Lord your God with all your heart,
with all your soul, with all your mind,
and with all your strength.

Mark 12:30

The challenge of loving God with all
our strength reminds me of those who are
slowly diminishing in all areas of physical
strength. In this portion of God's priority
command, I believe He is saying, "Love
Me with whatever physical strength you
have. Offer Me your temple for My full
habitation in weakness or in strength, in
living or in dying."

I watched my weak, dying mother
trying to move her lips to sing hymns with
me in her last hours. She loved God with
all her strength until He finally came and
lifted her burden from her. We love God
with all our strength when we give Him
all we have, however little or much.

And they will be called righteous trees,
planted by the Lord, to glorify Him.
Isaiah 61:3

If you're like me, you may be pretty excited about being set apart to "glorify Him," but you may not be all that thrilled about being called a tree. Yet captives set free are "oaks of righteousness" (NIV). The Hebrew word for "righteousness" means "honesty, integrity, liberation."

No matter what our strongholds have been, God can plant us deeply in His love, grow us by the water of His Word, and call us His "oaks of righteousness." We can be called people of honesty, integrity, and liberation—glorious results that come only to those who have allowed God to create in them a new and clean heart.

It is what I desire: to dwell in the
house of the Lord all the days of my life,
gazing on the beauty of the Lord.
Psalm 27:4

Imagine Christ boasting about how
beautiful you are because of the time
you've spent gazing on the "beauty of the
Lord." I don't know about you, but my
heart is leaping at the thought!

I am secure in God's love, even when
I'm not very beautiful, but the idea of
giving Him something to boast about
elates me! You see, the more we gaze on
the beauty of the Lord as we seek Him in
His temple, the more our lives absorb and
radiate His splendor. God's ultimate goal
is to display our portraits and say, "Doesn't
she look like My Son? A remarkable likeness, wouldn't you say?"

Let them present their witnesses
to vindicate themselves, so that people
may hear and say, "It is true."
Isaiah 43:9

This verse from Isaiah 43 states the primary purpose of a witness. It declares that our knowledge of and belief in God is never more beautiful than when others can look at our lives, hear our testimonies, and say, "It is true." That's what it means to be living proof!

If you bask in knowing God and dare to believe Him—whether or not you are even aware of the effectiveness of your testimony—I promise you that someone has seen truth through your witness. It is our reason for being here: to show forth the truth and glory of God.

Lord, I love the house where You dwell,
the place where Your glory resides.

Psalm 26:8

As I ask you the following question, please trust my heart toward you, because there is not a hint of judgment or condemnation, no matter what your answer. But do you presently have a yearning for the presence of God? I'm not talking about guilt feelings or even conviction of sin when He's not your priority. I'm referring to a yearning for God that makes only a few days without time in prayer and His Word seem like an eternity.

God can use any motivation to get us into His Word and prayer, but He wants to refine our motivations until they become a deep, yearning desire for Him.

August

The blood on the houses where you are staying
will be a distinguishing mark for you.
Exodus 12:13

When God instituted the Passover, He
already knew what the deliverance of His
children would cost. He knew He would
one day lay down the life of His own first-
born so that any captive, Jew or Gentile,
could be free.

But first, God demanded preparation
from His people. I believe the same is true
for us. God sent Christ to set the captives
free, but He undoubtedly demands our
attention and preparation. He wants us
never to forget that blood was shed by the
Lamb so we could be delivered. We have
no door of escape unless the doorpost has
been painted with the blood of Christ.

At daybreak, Lord, You hear my voice;
at daybreak I plead my case to You
and watch expectantly.

Psalm 5:3

Some days I want to forget I've ever been to Egypt. Some days I just want to act like I've always done it right. My times in Egypt are embarrassing for me to admit. Some days I think I just can't do it.

But each and every morning, the Holy Spirit woos me once again to the place where I meet with God. The God of grace bows low and meets with me. In the simplicity of my prayer time, I am suddenly confronted by the majesty of my Redeemer, the One who is responsible for any good in me. My past sins are forgiven, and fresh mercies fall like manna from heaven. Once again my heart is moved, and I surrender all. Morning after morning.

If you offer yourself to the hungry,
and satisfy the afflicted one, then your
light will shine in the darkness.
Isaiah 58:10

Usually we think of fasting as avoiding food for the purpose of prayer. The emptiness of our stomachs reminds us to pray. Although New Testament Scripture often speaks of fasting from food for this purpose, Isaiah 58 speaks of a fasting I believe God may honor most of all.

I've spent some time on this question, and I don't think it's an easy one to answer. What is God proposing that we fast from? What do we have to give up or fast from to reach out to the oppressed? Whatever our answer, we know if we pour out our lives to satisfy the needs of the oppressed, God will be faithful to satisfy our needs.

Lend, expecting nothing in return.
Then your reward will be great, and
you will be sons of the Most High.
Luke 6:35

Our motivations for reaching out and serving others aren't always pure. My dear friend Kathy Troccoli, who ministers full-time, asked a critical question: "Am I ministering out of my need, or out of the overflow of my own relationship with God?" We would be wise to ask ourselves the same question.

Do we crave the affirmation of those we serve? Do they help us feel important? Or do we serve because Jesus has so filled our hearts that we must find a place to pour out the overflow? A ministry to the truly oppressed helps to purify our serving motives, because these people don't have much to give back.

> Those who trust in the Lord
> will renew their strength.
> *Isaiah 40:31*

Sometimes I get tired of fighting the good fight, don't you? How can we muster the energy to hang in there and keep fighting for our liberty? Even the youth grow tired and weary, and young men stumble and fall. So what's a soul to do?

The Hebrew word for "trust" in the verse above means "to bind together (by twisting) . . . to be gathered together, to be joined." If we want to keep a renewed strength to face our daily challenges or to regain a strength that has faded, God's Word tells us to draw so close to the presence of God that we're practically twisted to Him!

Even though our outer person is being destroyed,
our inner person is being renewed day by day.
2 Corinthians 4:16

When my children were little, they used to hold on to my waist and wrap their legs around one of mine. I'd whistle, go about my business, and say, "I wonder what Amanda (or Melissa) is doing right now?" They would laugh hysterically. My heart never failed to be overwhelmed with love, because I realized that their favorite game was to hang on to me.

Who did most of the work in this game? I did. What was their part in it? Binding themselves to me and hanging on tight. Do you see the parallel? When we start feeling weary, we're probably taking on too much of the battle ourselves.

Because he was too afraid of
his father's household and the men
of the city . . . he did it at night.

Judges 6:27

To live in the kind of freedom God has purposed, you must recognize and forsake all other gods. As God told Gideon, "Tear down the altar of Baal that belongs to your father" (Judg. 6:25). But I love verse 27. Gideon took ten of his servants and did as the Lord said, but because he was afraid, "he did it at night" rather than the daytime. Don't you just love it? This is God's mighty warrior!

You are being asked now to do the same thing—to tear down any idols in your life, including those you didn't even know you had. But don't be afraid, because you don't even have to think of yourself as a "mighty warrior" to do it!

Satisfy us in the morning with
Your faithful love so that we may shout
with joy and be glad all our days.
Psalm 90:14

Searching for perfect, unfailing love in anyone else is not only fruitless, it is miserably disappointing and destructive. I am convinced our hearts are not healthy until they have been satisfied by the only completely healthy love that exists: the love of God Himself.

These words of Oswald Chambers are not only written in the front of my Bible, they are engraved deeply in my mind: "No love of the natural heart is safe unless the human heart has been satisfied by God first." We are not free to love in the true intent of the word until we have found love ourselves. In Him.

Love never fails.

1 Corinthians 13:8 (NIV)

We are not wrong to think we desperately need to be loved. We do. But we are wrong to think we can make anyone love us the way we need to be loved. Our need for love does not constitute anyone else's call but God's.

Perhaps you've heard the devastating words, "I just don't love you any more." Others may not have heard the words but have felt the feeling. Throughout life we will lose people—people who really loved us—to death or changing circumstances. As dear and rich as their love was, it was not unfailing. It moved. It died. It changed. It left wonderful memories, but it also left a hole. Only God's love never fails.

You have been filled by Him.

Colossians 2:10

No one is more pleasurable to be around than a person who has had her cup filled by the Lord Jesus Christ. He is the only One who is never overwhelmed by the depth and length of our need.

Imagine how different our days would be if we had our cups filled by Christ first thing in the morning. During the course of the day, anything else that anyone would be able to offer would just be the overflow of an already full cup. This person would never lack company or affection, because she draws daily from the well of unfailing love. She would know from experience what it means to be "filled by Him."

For the Lord has called you,
like a wife deserted and wounded in spirit.

Isaiah 54:6

I don't believe that rejection, in and of itself, is a stronghold. It's our *reaction* to rejection that determines whether or not we become bound by it.

Only God knows the number of His children who have allowed themselves to be imprisoned by continuing feelings of rejection for the rest of their lives. I would never imply that getting over it is easy, but I do believe it is possible for every single person who puts his or her heart and mind to it to overcome. Overcoming rejection is God's unquestionable will for your life if you belong to Him.

> I will place My residence among you,
> and I will not reject you.
>
> *Leviticus 26:11*

Jesus Christ will never leave you or forsake you. He will never cast you away. He is incapable of suddenly deciding He no longer wants you. If you have received God's Son as your Savior, nothing you can do will cause Him to reject you.

So believe what God's Word tells you about Him and about you. You are defined by the love and acceptance of the Creator and Sustainer of the universe. He happens to think you are worth loving and keeping. Find your identity in Him. Apply large doses of His love to your wounded heart. Let Him renew your mind until the rejected thinks like the *accepted*.

The one who conceals his sins
will not prosper, but whoever confesses
and renounces them will find mercy.
Proverbs 28:13

Nothing makes us feel more powerless than an addiction. But no matter whether your addictions are to substances or to behaviors, God can set you free. What He requires from you now is time, trust, and cooperation.

The immense power of an addiction is rarely broken in a day. You see, God has as much to *teach* us as He has to *show* us. He could show us His power by instantly setting us free from all desire for our stronghold. Often, however, God chooses the process of teaching us to walk with Him and depend on Him daily.

Lord, our God, other lords than You have ruled
over us, but we remember Your name alone.
Isaiah 26:13

Few things beyond our salvation are
"once and for all." If God were to deliver
us instantaneously from a stronghold or
addiction, we would see His greatness
once, but we would likely soon forget . . .
and we'd risk going back.

On the other hand, if God teaches us
victory in Jesus Christ day by day, then we
learn to live in the constant awareness of
His greatness and His sufficiency. Hard
lessons are often long-lasting lessons.

Never forget the fact that God is far
more interested in our getting to know the
Deliverer than in simply being delivered.

May the God of peace Himself
sanctify you completely.
1 Thessalonians 5:23

What a relief to know that we'll never battle anything out of God's jurisdiction. He can just as easily defeat His opposition on Mt. Carmel as He can on Mt. Zion. It's all His turf.

The same is true in regard to our own battlegrounds. God created us to be whole creatures made of three different components: body, soul, and spirit. So as long as we see God as Lord of our spirits alone, we will continue to live in areas of defeat.

God is as surely the Lord of our souls and bodies as He is of our spirits.

Choose for yourselves today
the one you will worship.

Joshua 24:15

The concept of rededicating our lives to Christ at infrequent revivals or conferences can prove disappointing. This verse from Joshua suggests a far more workable approach. Christ repeated the concept when He called us to take up our cross *daily* and follow Him.

A daily recommitment is not to ensure that we'll never fail, but to help us develop the mentality that every single day is a new day—a new chance to follow Christ. Obedience to God is not some diet we suddenly blow. It is something to which we recommit every single day, no matter how we blew it the day before.

> The accuser of our brothers has been
> thrown out: the one who accuses them
> before our God day and night.
> *Revelation 12:10*

The acceptance of God's forgiveness through Jesus Christ swings our prison doors wide open. And Satan knows that whatever God opens, no one can close (Rev. 3:7). So if he is powerless to shut our prison doors, what is Satan's next best option? He can convince us to stay, even though we've been freed to leave.

One of his primary methods of keeping us pinned by our own volition in our prison cells is *accusation*. He is the master of accusation. Because he wants what Christ has—and knows he can't have it—he attempts to counterfeit and counteract everything Christ does. He is our accuser.

> The Son of Man has
> authority on earth to forgive sins.
> *Luke 5:24*

Never in all of Scripture does Christ resist the repentant sinner. He resisted the proud and the self-righteous religious, but never the humble and repentant. Indeed, forgiveness is why He came.

When we approach God in genuine repentance, taking full responsibility for our own sins, our prison doors swing open. Tragically, we can sit right there in our prison cells for years and years by refusing or not knowing to stand on God's promises and walk forward in His truth. And since Satan knows that forgiveness leads to freedom, he will do everything he can to see that we don't forgive ourselves. But Christ has already forgiven us.

Godly grief produces a repentance
not to be regretted and leading to salvation,
but worldly grief produces death.
2 Corinthians 7:10

I remember a time in my college years when I was deeply puzzled over ongoing feelings of guilt concerning a sin for which I had asked forgiveness many, many times. I never felt like I was out from under the weight and burden of it.

Years later, God pried open my eyes to the verse above. Suddenly I realized that I had never developed a godly sorrow over that sin. I *regretted* it because I knew it wasn't God's will for my life, but I had no real sorrow over it. I had hung on to it emotionally even though I had let go of it physically. I had *done* the right things, but I still *felt* the wrong things.

If our hearts condemn us, God is greater
than our hearts and knows all things.
1 John 3:20

I cannot count the times believers have
come to me in the last decade and told me
that they had turned from a sinful relationship, but could not seem to let go of
the emotional tie. They were still cherish-
ing the sin in their hearts (Ps. 66:18).
Godly sorrow is not defined by tears or
outward displays of contrition. Rather, it's
a change of heart resulting in complete
agreement with God over the matter.

You may say, "Beth, I can't change the
way I feel." I understand. I've been there.
But that's why it's called godly sorrow. It's
a work of God. He can change our hearts,
because He is "greater than our hearts."

When the devil had finished all this tempting,
he left him until an opportune time.

Luke 4:13 (NIV)

After traveling and talking to so many
believers in various crises and strongholds,
I am convinced that we are giving Satan
far too much credit for having some sem-
blance of heart. Please understand, Satan
has no heart.

We find a strange, deceptive comfort
in imagining that Satan would draw the
line at certain limits and act appropriately.
For instance, we mistakenly assume that
surely Satan would leave us alone in our
heart-rending grief because, after all, he
knows we're defenseless and weak. *Wrong.*
Satan is an opportunist. Would he come
after you while you are down? In a heart-
beat . . . if he had a heart.

Why do you spend money on what is not food,
and your wages on what does not satisfy?

Isaiah 55:2

Have you ever noticed that one of the most common human experiences is the inability for us to be completely satisfied? Unfortunately, salvation by itself doesn't completely fill the need.

Many come to Christ out of their search for something missing. Yet after receiving salvation, they go elsewhere for further satisfaction.

Christians can be miserably dissatisfied if they accept Christ's salvation yet reject the fullness of daily relationship that satisfies. God offers us so much more than we usually choose to enjoy.

Humble yourselves therefore
under the mighty hand of God, so that
He may exalt you in due time.

1 Peter 5:6

Humility is not something we have
until humbling ourselves is something we
do. This step necessitates action before
possession. Humbling ourselves certainly
does not mean hating ourselves. Humility
can be rather easily obtained by opening
our eyes to reality—filling our minds and
hearts with the greatness of God.

That's what humility is in a nutshell:
bowing down before His power and
majesty. We don't have to hang our heads
in demeaning self-abasement. We must
simply choose to lower our heads from
lofty, inappropriate places. We choose to
humble ourselves by submitting to His
greatness every day.

He is able to humble those who walk in pride.
Daniel 4:37

This phrase from Daniel 4:37 provides one of the most effective motivations for humility in my personal life. I look at it this way: I'd rather humble myself than force God to humble me.

Let's allow our circumstances and weaknesses, as well as any thorns in the flesh God has chosen to leave, to do the job they were sent to do—provoke humility. Not so we can be flattened under God's doormat, but so He can joyfully lift us up. Take a moment today to get down on your knees and humble yourself before your glorious God. The hosts of heaven are sure to hear a thunderous rumble as boulders of pride roll off our road to freedom.

> God's foolishness is wiser than
> human wisdom, and God's weakness
> is stronger than human strength.
> *1 Corinthians 1:25*

Recently, I again saw the best advice the world seems to have: "Just remember two things: 1) Don't sweat the small stuff. 2) It's all small stuff." This advice is so shallow. It's *not* all small stuff.

I have a friend whose son was paralyzed in an accident his senior year in high school. I have seen hardworking men lose their jobs. I have watched tornadoes whip through my hometown—stealing, killing, and destroying. But worldly philosophy is forced to minimize difficulty because it has no real answers to it. You and I know better. We face a lot of big stuff out there. And only through prayer are we washed in peace.

He will pray to God, and God will
delight in him. That man will behold
His face with a shout of joy.

Job 33:26

We need prayer as we seek to break
free, because Satan will try to stir up what
our faithful Refiner wants to skim off.
Remember, Christ came to set the captive
free; Satan comes to make the free captive.
Christ wants to cut some binding ropes
from our lives; Satan will want to use
them to tie us in knots.

So we must walk with Christ step-by-
step through this journey for the sake of
protection, power, and the unparalleled
passion that results from it. None of these
three things will be realities in our lives
any other way. The enemy will be defeated.
Believe it. Act on it.

> In order to accuse Him, they asked Him,
> "Is it lawful to heal on the Sabbath?"
> *Matthew 12:10*

Modern-day Pharisees are still fond of practicing religious voyeurism, looking for a reason to accuse others. They tend to love a church "soap opera," primarily because their own relationship with God is so unexciting. They look to the faults of others to keep things interesting.

I have unfortunately seen many caring Christians intimidated by the occasional legalist, those who concentrate on the shortcomings of others and try to cheat believers from truly enjoying the presence of God. Be careful of those who allow microscopes to replace mirrors in their lives, holding you to standards you were never called to maintain.

Let the peace of the Messiah, to which you were
also called in one body, control your hearts.
Colossians 3:15

What does it take to have this peace?
Attention to God's command (obedience)
through the power of the Holy Spirit.
Obedience to God's authority not only
brings peace like a river but righteousness
like the waves of the sea. Not righteous
perfection, but righteous consistency.

You see, God's way is the safe way, the
right way, and the only peaceful way in
our chaotic world. I hope you're discover-
ing that peace is not beyond your reach.
It's not a goal to meet one day. You can
begin a life of authentic peace right now.
But the path to peace is paved with knee-
prints. Bend your knee to the trustworthy
authority of Christ.

> We have this treasure in clay jars,
> so that this extraordinary power may
> be from God and not from us.
> *2 Corinthians 4:7*

Here is my personal checklist of Scriptures and evaluations that I seek to apply to my life on a regular basis:

- Is my most important consideration in every undertaking whether or not God could be glorified? (1 Cor. 10:31)
- Do I desire God's glory or my own? (John 8:50, 54)
- In my service to others, is my sincere hope that they will somehow see God in me? (1 Pet. 4:10–11)
- When I am going through hardships, do I turn to God and try to cooperate with Him so He can use them for my good and for His glory? (1 Pet. 4:12–13).

All My things are Yours, and Yours are Mine,
and I have been glorified in them.
John 17:10

You may feel like you have a long way to go before you are fulfilling His purpose. But I hope you can celebrate the progress you are making in your pursuit of a God-glorifying life, and can relish these words of Christ that pertain to you.

In this context, Jesus used the word "glorified" to indicate wealth and riches He had received. No matter where you are on the journey to a glorifying, liberated life in Christ, you are His treasure. He does not want to *take* from you. He wants to *give* to you and to free you from every hindrance that threatens you.

I am jealous over you with a godly jealousy.
2 Corinthians 11:2

I know a little of what the apostle Paul meant when he spoke these words to the church in Corinth. My friend, I am truly "jealous" for you to enjoy God. I want Him to be the greatest reality in your life. I want you to be more assured of His presence than of anyone else's you can see or touch.

This can be your reality. This is your right as a child of God. We were destined for this kind of relationship with Him, even though the enemy tries to convince us that the Christian life is sacrificial at best and artificial at worst. Commit yourself entirely to God, that He may set you free to be everything He planned.

September

Let us lay aside every weight and the sin
that so easily ensnares us, and run with
endurance the race that lies before us.
Hebrews 12:1

The longer I've walked with God in
prayer and His Word and have come to
love Him, the less I want Him to let me off
easy. I'm learning that a believer's willingness to do "the hard thing" is what sets
him or her apart for the extraordinary in
Christ.

I'm beginning to learn to say, "Lord,
my flesh is so resistant to what You want
right now that I can hardly stand it. But
don't stop! Insist upon my best. Insist
upon Your glory. Take me up to the line
on this, God. Don't let up on me until
we've gone every inch of the distance."

We are ambassadors for Christ; certain that
God is appealing through us, we plead on
Christ's behalf: "Be reconciled to God."
2 Corinthians 5:20

No matter how different the rest of
our challenges may be, every believer can
count on a multitude of challenges to
forgive.

Remember, God's primary agenda in
the life of the believer is to conform the
child into the likeness of His Son, Jesus
Christ. And no other word sums up His
character in relationship to us like the
word *forgiving*. We never look more like
Him than when we forgive. And since this
is God's goal for us, we're destined for
plenty of opportunities! As ambassadors
of Christ in this generation, we have been
called to the ministry of forgiveness.

I sank to the foundations of the mountains;
the earth with its prison bars closed behind me
forever! But You raised my life from the Pit.
Jonah 2:6

I believe I can confidently and reverently say to you that God can put any broken person back together again, no matter what he or she has suffered. I'm not just saying that God can cause a person to maintain his or her physical existence after tragedy. Many people *live* through tragedy.

Physical existence is not what Christ died to bring us. He came that we might have life and have it more abundantly. As impossible and unreachable as this truth may seem, God can restore abundant life. For now, you may just need to keep breathing, but you can learn to live once again.

Although these have a reputation of wisdom
by promoting ascetic practices . . . they are not
of any value against fleshly indulgence.
Colossians 2:23

If man could truly subdue all his fleshly
appetites by the pure power of his own
determination, he would simply worship
his own will. But if the Word of God is
about anything at all, it is about God's
will rather than ours. Our liberty is para-
doxically discovered through the will of
God rather than our own.

Through the might of the Holy Spirit,
we are empowered to say "no" to things
we should—our excesses, withholdings,
compulsions, and other harmful consump-
tions—and "yes" to freedom, moderation,
and better health. When we bow to God's
authority, we invite Him to take control,
and He is the one who does it.

Instead, he took his staff in his hand and
chose five small stones. . . . Then with his sling
in his hand, he approached the Philistine.
1 Samuel 17:40

Realize that God's unquestionable will
for you is your freedom from the yoke,
but also trust that He has written a person-
alized prescription for your release.

God may have used a method to set
someone else free that doesn't work as
effectively for you. Perhaps the success of
others has done little more than increase
your discouragement and self-hatred. But
don't let the enemy play mind games with
you. God's strength is tailor-made for
weakness. We are never stronger than the
moment when we admit we are weak.
Seek God diligently and ask Him to show
you the way to victory.

The Lord will not abandon His people,
because of His great name and because He has
determined to make you His own people.
1 Samuel 12:22

Someone who has never experienced
rejection might wonder whether or not it's
a serious form of suffering. However, if
you've been rejected by someone you love,
you'll agree that few injuries are more
excruciating.

So take heart in this: God was pleased
to make you His own. Pleased! He didn't
just feel sorry for you. He wasn't obligated
to you. He chose you because He delights
in you. You were never meant to get
through life by the skin of your teeth. You
were meant to flourish in the love and
acceptance of Almighty Jehovah. When
He sings over you, dance!

I have chosen the way of truth;
I have set Your ordinances before me.
Psalm 119:30

Sometimes we're very aware of tolerating or even fueling a lie. Other times, we are caught in such a web that we can no longer see ourselves or our situations with any sense of accuracy.

It's not always clear when we're being deceived, but one sure sign is when we ourselves are beginning to deceive. All you have to do to locate Satan in any situation is to look for the lie.

How do we recognize a lie? Anything that we are believing or acting on that is contrary to what the truth of God's Word says about us is a lie.

We have renounced shameful
secret things, not walking in deceit
or distorting God's message.
2 Corinthians 4:2

Satan's plans toward the believer are always the antithesis of God's plans. The Lord wants to loose us from the closets of secrecy and bring us to a spacious place of joy, freedom, authenticity, and transparency. Satan wants to keep us bound in secrecy where he can weigh us down in guilt, misery, and shame.

Oh, beloved, I know from experience that so much of the shame we allow ourselves to endure in life is wrapped up in the secret. In fact, the enemy knows that once we expose the secret places of our lives to the light of God's Word, we're on our way to freedom.

He has rescued us from the domain
of darkness and transferred us into the
kingdom of the Son He loves.

Colossians 1:13

I have surrendered my life to a very radical walk with God, but I'm not miserable about it, nor do I fight the feeling that "this is what I get for being defeated by the devil all my life." I have come to a place where I usually delight to do God's will, and I see His precepts for me as green lights for victory, peace, joy, fullness, and passion.

Yes, I was forced to make some radical decisions. Perhaps you will be, too. But I wouldn't trade the relationship with Christ that I discovered in my desperation for all the spotless track records in the world. Neither should you.

You are from God, little children, and you have
conquered them, because the One who is in you
is greater than the one who is in the world.

1 John 4:4

I never want to go back to my life of
defeat. I live in alertness daily. However,
God used my defeat to bring me to a place
of ministry and authenticity I would never
have known. It was not until I was broken
that God was released to create in me a
healthy heart and teach me the humility
and compassion of a true servant.

I have a long way to go, but I have put
the devil on notice: he may make my life
very difficult, but he cannot make me quit.
For I, like you, am one of God's dear children, and I have overcome the spirits of
darkness because the One who is in me is
greater than the one who is in the world.

Though it delays, wait for it,
since it will certainly come and not be late.
Habakkuk 2:3

Single person: if you are in Christ, you have the ultimate relationship ahead of you. If God calls you to a life of singleness, feel special, and save yourself entirely for Him!

Husband or wife with common frustrations: give your spouse room to be human. Forgive him for not being God. Forgive her for not always saying what you need to hear.

Until the ultimate relationship arrives, let your mirror image be the face of Christ. Your bridal portrait is being painted one day at a time.

> I have learned to be content
> in whatever circumstances I am.
> *Philippians 4:11*

We've all known people who claimed they'd be happy if only they were married, had children, had a big house, or had the right job. But most people who are banking on circumstantial contentment will find themselves in emotional bankruptcy sooner or later.

Unhappy people are not made happy by marriage, by children, or by any other possession they don't have at the moment. An unhappy person usually needs a change of heart more than a change of circumstances. I don't believe God will allow surrendered hearts to continue to long for things He will not ultimately grant in one way or another.

Let us shout for joy at your victory
and lift the banner in the name of our God.
Psalm 20:5

I believe we can draw three conclusions about strongholds:

1) Every stronghold is related to something we have exalted to a higher position than God in our lives.

2) Every stronghold pretends to bring us something we feel we must have: aid, comfort, the relief of stress, protection, or some other perceived benefit.

3) Every stronghold in the life of the believer is a tremendous source of pride for the enemy.

Let this make you mad enough at him to stop giving him the satisfaction.

Consecrate yourselves, because the Lord
will do wonders among you tomorrow.
Joshua 3:5

We're all looking for a quick fix, but
God is after lasting change—a lifestyle of
Christianity. To *possess* a steadfast mind
is to *practice* a steadfast mind. You and I
have been controlled and held prisoner by
destructive, negative, misleading thoughts
for too long. Through the divine power of
the Holy Spirit, we can take our thoughts
prisoner instead!

Remember, this is a war for freedom,
and the battlefield is the mind. That's why
Joshua's exhortation to the children of
Israel applies so beautifully to us. The
wonders God wants to do in all our tomor-
rows are prepared for in our todays.

Everyone who competes
exercises self-control in everything.
1 Corinthians 9:25

I'm not being overly dramatic when I say we can either tear down our strongholds with the mighty power of God or they will eventually tear us down.

We don't even have to love something or someone to idolize or exalt it in our minds. We can easily idolize something we hate! I'll never forget realizing that a person I felt I couldn't forgive had become an idol to me through my unforgiveness. Humanly speaking, I didn't even like the person, yet Satan had seized my imagination until the whole situation stole my focus and therefore became idolatrous to me. May it never be so. Let God have the victory in everything!

I say then, walk by the Spirit and you
will not carry out the desire of the flesh.
Galatians 5:16

Staying at work on our thought life is
the very essence of godliness. Godliness is
not perfection. If you are striving daily to
give God your heart and mind and are
sensitive to sin in your thought life, I'd
call you godly. But I could never call myself
that. Maybe that's how it should be.

Here's a rule of thumb for the thought
life that will be a catalyst for victory in all
parts of life: *starve the flesh* and *feed the
spirit*. These phrases were pivotal for me,
and I hope they will be for you, too. On
every day that the believer practices these
principles, victory will be the rule and
defeat the exception in her life.

> He brought me to the banquet hall,
> and he looked on me with love.
> *Song of Songs 2:4*

God often teaches the unknown through the known. I believe the Song of Songs was written to help us relate to our union with Christ. In this book we can see Christ and His beloved bride—us. Real romance awaits all of us. Single and married people alike can celebrate that some dreams will really come true.

One of them is perfectly portrayed in this inspired book of the Bible. Christ is completely taken with you. He sees you as His beloved, His bride. Have you ever longed to be truly loved? Jesus waves His hand over you, signaling to all in sight that you are the one He loves.

You turned my lament into dancing;
You removed my sackcloth and
clothed me with gladness.
Psalm 30:11

Meditate on the word "gladness" for a moment. If anybody in the world should experience gladness, it should be Christians! But what if we pressed the concept a tad further? I'd like to suggest that God enjoys seeing us—dare I say—happy?

Believe it or not, *happy* is a biblical word, although we are wise to distinguish it from two closely associated words in Scripture—*blessing* and *joy*. Both blessing and joy come to us through obedience, often in times of persecution and pain. The obvious difference is that blessing and joy are not circumstantial, while happiness is. This doesn't make happiness lesser, however, just rarer.

> The time will come when they will
> not tolerate sound doctrine.
> *2 Timothy 4:3*

A rebellious child prefers pleasant illusions over truth. We crave messages that make us feel good. When we are living in rebellion, the last thing we want is to confront the Holy One of Israel.

So the apostle Paul was right in his warning to young Timothy. If we strongly prefer certain teachers and preachers over others, we are wise to ask why. If our basis is anything other than balanced biblical teaching, we could be in rebellion while occupying our pews every Sunday. Let's make sure we are not looking for people to scratch our itching ears and hide us from the truth.

For you are called to freedom, brothers.
Galatians 5:13

Freedom and lordship are inseparable partners in the believer's life. When we read in the Scripture that freedom can be found anywhere the Spirit of the Lord is, we can take that literally.

Freedom becomes our reality when we yield to the authority of God. We are as filled with the Spirit as we are yielded to His lordship.

Although the Spirit of the living God is always in us, He floods only the parts of our lives where He is in full authority. Freedom flows everywhere the Spirit of the Lord floods.

The prisoner is soon to be set free;
he will not die and go to the Pit.
Isaiah 51:14

Have you felt like the waves of the sea were pounding against you, and you were drowning in a relentless tide? The prophet Isaiah reminds you that God can do for you what He did for Moses. He can make the "sea-bed into a road for the redeemed to pass over" (Isa. 51:10).

And have you ever felt like a cowering prisoner? I have! Have you ever felt like you would never be released? That's why I love Isaiah's words from verse 14 above. Believe God's Word and claim it! Obey and see that you can trust Him. Do not allow the enemy another success at using your past record against you.

The Lord is for me; I will not be afraid.
What can man do to me?
Psalm 118:6

Fellow sojourner, God has the right to rule. But better yet, God's rule is right! He cannot ask anything wrong of us, nor can He mislead us. He knows every authority problem we have. He knows the times when our trust has been betrayed.

And so like a father cupping his rebellious child's face in his strong hands, He says, "Listen to me . . . hear me . . . I, even I, am he who comforts you . . . I am the Lord your God" (Isa. 51:1, 7, 12, 15 NIV). Essentially, God is saying to us, "I am *for* you, child, not *against* you! When will you cease resisting Me?"

Rise up! Help us!
Redeem us because of Your faithful love.
Psalm 44:26

No doubt, each of us can think of a
few ways God allows the rebellious to
stumble. When I was a teenager, I could
have accepted the little truth I knew, but I
didn't. I not only stumbled; I crashed and
burned! And I am so thankful. Had I never
fallen, I don't know that I would have
cried out for help.

So how I thank Jesus for His unfailing
love to make sure others "failed" in their
attempts to help me! Sounds strange,
doesn't it? But I believe most of us would
never acknowledge God as God alone if
we didn't experience a crisis when no one
else could help. He never forsakes us.

His divine power has given us everything
required for life and godliness.
2 Peter 1:3

Finding satisfaction in God is one of
the chief benefits of our covenant relationship with Christ. Finding satisfaction and
fullness in Christ was never meant to be a
secret treasure that only a few could find.
Satisfaction is a blessed by-product of our
relationship with God, and it is meant for
every believer.

Peter expressed God's intention clearly
in this verse for today. God has given us
"everything . . . through the knowledge of
Him who called us by His own glory and
goodness." So either Christ can satisfy us
and meet our deepest needs, or God's
Word is deceptive.

Flee from sexual immorality!
1 Corinthians 6:18

None of us will question that Satan is having a field day in our generation in the area of sexual strongholds. His attacks have become so outright and blatant that we've become desensitized, unknowingly readjusting our plumb line to a state of relativity. Instead of measuring our lives against the goal of Christlikeness, we are beginning to subconsciously measure them against the world's depravity.

We are wise to be alert to the venomous snakebite of relativism. Satan is upping the dosage of sexually immoral provocation with such consistency, we don't realize how much poison we're swallowing.

> Can a man embrace fire
> and his clothes not be burned?
>
> *Proverbs 6:27*

The rate of Christians being snared daily in sexual strongholds is staggering. Satan gets his pawns trapped in secret shame, living miserable lives of deception. Please read this carefully: *we are being sexually assaulted by the devil.* And the church must start mentioning the unmentionable, biblically addressing the issues that are attacking our generation.

That's because God's Word applies to the strongholds of promiscuity, perversity, and pornography just as it does to any other. God is not shocked. He has the remedy for these. And He is awaiting our humble, earnest cry for help.

Repent and turn from all your transgressions,
so they will not be a stumbling block
that causes your punishment.
Ezekiel 18:30

One reliable rod for measuring close-ness to God would be the time that lapses between sin and repentance. The spiritual man still sins, but he cannot bear to resist immediate repentance. His overwhelming sensitivity to his own failure results in a holier life because he repents in the early stages of what would otherwise become a contagion of sin.

Indeed, those who walk most closely with God frustrate the best efforts of the accuser. By the time he arrives in the heav-enlies to register his accusations, God can say with pleasure, "I have no memory of that sin."

If you are ridiculed for the name of Christ,
you are blessed, because the Spirit of
glory and of God rests on you.

1 Peter 4:14

Satan employs no small list of willing
humans to add volume to his harsh, accusing voice in our lives. That's because he
knows that we are by nature a merciless,
condemning lot, eager to put others down.
I'm convinced that far more people would
burn in eternal flames under man's own
judgment than under that of a holy and
righteous God.

I urge you to know the truth of God
so thoroughly and respond to conviction
so readily that when accusations come—
as they inevitably will—you can resist the
devil, no matter whose voice grants him
volume.

One of His disciples, the one Jesus loved,
was reclining close beside Jesus.
John 13:23

The fear or the feeling of being unloved
is probably our greatest source of insecurity, whether or not we are always able to
articulate it. But how can we abide in the
love of God, even when other loves have
failed us? We must dwell closely to His
side, where we are most keenly aware of
His great affection.

Was it not the disciple who reclined
against Jesus who saw himself as the
"beloved disciple"? Place your ear against
the chest of the Savior so that, when trou-
bled times come and you don't know what
will befall you, you can hear the steady
pulse of Christ's boundless love.

He gathers the lambs in His arms and
carries them in the fold of His garment.

Isaiah 40:11

What a heavy yoke is shattered when
we awaken in the morning, bring our
hearts, minds, and souls and all their needs
to the Great Soul-ologist, offer Him our
empty cups, and ask Him to fill them with
Himself!

But what heartbreak we must bring to
God when we continue to disbelieve His
love. What more could He have said?
What more could He have done?

Believe even when you do not feel.
Know even when you do not see. He gave
the life of His Son to demonstrate His love
and power. The time has come to believe.

October

Only goodness and faithful love
will pursue me all the days of my life.
Psalm 23:6

God told King Hezekiah he was going to die, but Hezekiah turned his face to the wall and cried out to God. In response, God added fifteen years to the king's life.

But no sooner had he recovered than he started sounding as if his close encounter with death came with an automatic doctorate, as if the decision to spare one of God's own has anything to do with loving one person more than another. God cannot love us more or less than He does at this moment. He chooses to heal and not to heal for His own reasons. All His decisions come from His love. But whether He chooses to heal or take us home, His love remains constant.

> Speak tenderly to Jerusalem, and
> announce to her that her time of servitude
> is over, her iniquity has been pardoned.
> *Isaiah 40:2*

Chapters 40–66 begin a new theme in
the book of Isaiah. In these final chapters
of his prophecy, he spoke of a time when
the captivity of the people would end.
Israel would be comforted by God and
restored to her appointed purpose.

I love the way God worded the clear
turning point in Isaiah 40:1 after so many
chapters of declaring Israel's grievous sins
and chastisements. "'Comfort, comfort
My people,' says your God." It was time
for Him to "speak tenderly" to His children. Oh, how I thank Him for tender
words He has spoken to me after I have
been chastened for sin. I wonder why He
continues to be so faithful.

You saw the oppression of our ancestors
in Egypt and heard their cry at the Red Sea.
Nehemiah 9:9

God initiated the saving relationship
between the people and the Liberator. He
is intimately acquainted with the sorrows
and suffering that result from slavery. He
also has a remedy. He is the meeter of our
needs.

For all who have been taken captive,
God has sent a Deliverer. His liberating
words toward the people of Israel in the
Old Testament apply just as much to us as
they did in their day. In fact, His words of
comfort and rescue will continue to apply
as long as God looks down from the height
of His sanctuary, views the earth, and
hears the groaning of the prisoner.

> Then Jesus returned to Galilee
> in the power of the Spirit.
> *Luke 4:14*

Jesus knew the strain and struggle of temptation. We know how He famously withstood the enemy's appeals for Him to exercise His power for His own ends and before His appointed time. He remained obedient nonetheless. Then the Gospel of Luke records that "after the Devil had finished every temptation, he departed from Him for a time" (Luke 4:13).

But how encouraging to know that because the Spirit of God dwells in us, we too can come out of temptation "in the power of the Spirit"—more empowered than ever—maintaining our freedom as we learn to live in His power day-to-day.

You are My witnesses . . . and My servant
whom I have chosen, so that you may know and
believe Me and understand that I am He.
Isaiah 43:10

Did you note in this verse why we
have been "chosen" as His witnesses and
servants? It's so that we may "know" and
"believe" Him. The Hebrew word for
"know" is *yadha*, an ancient term that
encompassed a personal level of familiarity and was often used to depict the close
relationship between a husband and wife.

Yes, one of your chief purposes on this
planet is to know God intimately and with
reverent familiarity. That's why you should
often look back and say, "And I thought I
knew and loved Him before." This relationship of ours is designed to grow more
and more intimate over time.

Not that I have already reached the goal
or am already fully mature . . .
Philippians 3:12

Like me, you're probably overwhelmed by the enormous responsibility of our calling to bear Christ's name and reflect His glory. We're imperfect creatures! How are we supposed to help others recognize something of God just from their watching our lives and knowing us?

Sure, we've all fallen short and missed the mark in many, many ways. But anyone who knows our God knows He is far too tenacious to be thwarted by our sin. Jesus Christ Himself dwells in the life of every believer, and we are able to glorify Him to the degree that we externalize the internal existence of the living Christ.

He has shone in our hearts to
give the light of the knowledge of
God's glory in the face of Jesus Christ.
2 Corinthians 4:6

• We were created for God's glory,
created for the purpose of giving Christ's
invisible character a glimpse of visibility.

• We fulfill what we were meant to be
when God is recognizable in us.

• However, we have no hope of God's
glory if not for the indwelling Spirit of
Christ that comes to us at salvation.

• After that, a life that glorifies God or
makes Him recognizable is a process that
ideally progresses with time and maturity.

If we grasp the eternal consequences
of such a destiny, we would want to do
anything possible to make sure all our
hindrances are removed in order to glorify
Him daily and faithfully.

He satisfies you with goodness;
your youth is renewed like the eagle.
Psalm 103:5

Many Christians are not satisfied with Jesus. Before you call me a heretic, let me set the record straight: *Jesus is absolutely satisfying.* In fact, He is the only means by which any mortal creature can find true satisfaction. However, I believe a person can receive Christ as Savior, serve Him for decades, and even meet Him face-to-face in glory without ever experiencing satisfaction in Him.

Please understand that there's a huge difference between salvation from sin and satisfaction of soul. Salvation secures our lives for all eternity. Soul satisfaction ensures abundant life on earth.

> As He approached and saw the city,
> He wept over it, saying, "If you knew this
> day what would bring peace . . ."
> *Luke 19:41–42*

Jesus weeps over us until we learn how to activate His peace. The Greek word for "wept" in this verse is the strongest word for grief used in the New Testament. And although Jesus wept on several occasions in Scripture, this is the only occasion where His grief is described by this particularly intense word. He deeply desires that we experience His peace.

For me, I've found that I can't retain peace in the present and rely on a relationship from the past. As a river is continually renewed with the moving waters of springs and streams, so our peace comes from an active, ongoing, and obedient relationship with the Prince of Peace.

Even the darkness is not dark to You.
The night shines like the day.

Psalm 139:12

God's Word often tells us not to fear, yet not all of our fears are unfounded. Think about it. Our present society poses many real threats that are far from being figments of our imaginations, and Christians are not exempt from being caught up in the crossfire. The Bible doesn't tell us to trust Him "if" we pass through the waters, but "when."

So God is not suggesting that difficult things don't happen to His children. But if nothing frightening ever happened to us, how could the assurance of God's constant presence still be the quieter of our fears? His presence in our lives is unchanging, even when the evidence of it is not.

Immediately Jesus spoke to them.
"Have courage! It is I. Don't be afraid."
Matthew 14:27

When Jesus spoke these words to His disciples while walking on the water, the storm continued to rage. The point is not that we have nothing to fear, but that His presence is the basis for our courage.

No, Christ does not always calm the storm immediately, but He is always willing to calm His child on the basis of His presence. "Don't worry!" he says. "I know the winds are raging and the waves are high, but I am God over both. If I let them continue to swell, it's because I want you to see Me walk on the water." We'll probably never learn to enjoy our storms, but we can learn to enjoy God's presence in the midst of them.

You give him blessings forever;
You cheer him with joy in Your presence.
Psalm 21:6

Before we can begin to enjoy God's presence in our lives, we must accept His continual presence in our lives as an absolute fact. Are you one who needs a set of prints for reassurance? The most wonderful set of fingerprints God has left with His invisible hand is probably within your reach this very moment: His Word.

Scripture declares to us that God never abandons His children. He is always there. When it all comes down, we choose either to believe or disbelieve God. But once we choose to accept His presence as an established fact, then we can be free to move on to enjoyment.

The One on the throne said,
"Look, I am making everything new."
Revelation 21:5

As much as I enjoy my husband, my daughters, my family, and my friends, no relationship in my life brings me more joy than my relationship with God. I certainly haven't "arrived" in some mystical place, nor have I made even these few steps quickly or casually. I've grown to enjoy God over time. Not every moment I spend with Him is gleeful or great fun.

But intimacy with God grows through sharing every realm of experience. Weeping bitterly. Screaming in frustration. Laughing out loud. Squealing in excitement. Dropping to our knees in worship. Jesus is life. All of life.

Now is the judgment of this world.
Now the ruler of this world will be cast out.
John 12:31

The enemy has no right to hold you back from realizing any of the benefits God has promised you in His Word. They are yours. And yet, it's quite likely that you are vividly aware today of an area of real captivity in your life.

I urge you to come before God with boldness today, asking Him in Jesus' name not to let the enemy steal one bit of the victory God has for you. We must not allow intimidation or fear to imprison us in any area. Remember, Satan can presume no authority in your life. He will do his best to bluff you. Don't let him. Instead, listen closely. The liberty bell is ringing.

This is the work of God:
that you believe in the One He has sent.
John 6:29

You may have been battling an area of captivity for a very long time. Or you may not have a clue about what is holding you back from the full benefit of your salvation. You may have almost given up on ever experiencing the reality of abundant life. Somewhere along the way, you may have simply ceased believing God is able.

But if you're willing to admit your lack of confidence in Him, Christ is more than willing to help you overcome your unbelief. Faith in the abilities and promises of God is a vital prerequisite for fleshing out the liberty we've won through Jesus Christ.

God is not a man who lies, or the son of
man who changes His mind. Does He speak
and not act, or promise and not fulfill?

Numbers 23:19

Can you think of a time when God
proved unworthy of your confidence? If
we think we've discovered unfaithfulness
in God, I believe one of three things has
happened: 1) we misinterpreted the promise, 2) we missed the answer, or 3) we gave
up before God timed His response.

We must simply keep believing Him,
because unbelief is crippling, casting huge
obstacles in the way of a victorious life.
The steps we take forward with God, we
take through faith. This doesn't mean He
asks us to believe in our ability to exercise
unwavering faith. He merely asks us to
believe that He is able.

Immediately the father of the boy cried out,
"I do believe! Help my unbelief."
Mark 9:24

If you are having difficulty believing
you really could live out the liberty of
Christ, would you make the same plea the
father made to Jesus in Mark 9:24? Spend
some time in prayer asking the Father to
overcome your unbelief.

The apostle Paul said it best: "I know
whom I have believed and am persuaded
that He is able to guard what has been
entrusted to me until that day" (2 Tim.
1:12). We tend to run to God for temporary relief. God is looking for people who
will walk with Him in steadfast belief. So
choose to believe. Those who trust in Him
will never be put to shame.

Our desire is for Your name and renown.
Isaiah 26:8

God is glorified in any of His people through whom He is allowed to show Himself great or mighty. So how can we be assured of living a God-glorifying life? By adopting a God-glorifying attitude.

We are called to allow the King of all creation to reveal Himself through us. He will not share His glory with another, not even with His own children—not because He's outrageously egotistical, but because He's interested in our eternal treasures. By demanding that we seek His glory alone, He calls us to overcome the overwhelming and natural temptation to seek our own. The way to true joy and identity is found in treasuring His "name and renown."

I will leave a meek and humble people among
you, and they will trust in the name of Yahweh.
Zephaniah 3:12

God wants to get to our hearts, but
pride covers the heart. God wants to free
us from any hindrances in our past, but
pride refuses to take a fresh look back.
God wants to treat us with the prescription of His Word, but pride doesn't like to
be told what to do.

God wants to bring us out of dark
closets, but pride says our secrets are
nobody's business. God wants to help us
with constraining problems, but pride
denies there *is* a problem. God wants to
make us strong in Him, but pride won't
admit to weakness. Take it from someone
who knows the reality of captivity: pride
inhibits the journey to freedom.

Your presumptuous heart has deceived you.
Obadiah 3

Proverbs 8:13 quotes God as saying, "I hate arrogant pride." Proverbs 11:2 proclaims, "When pride comes, disgrace follows, but with humility comes wisdom." Proverbs 13:10 adds, "Arrogance leads to nothing but strife, but wisdom is gained by those who take advice." And in the familiar words of Proverbs 16:18, "Pride comes before destruction, and an arrogant spirit before a fall."

Let me see . . . God hates it, it brings disgrace, it breeds quarrels, and it points us to destruction like a compass needle seeking north. The first shove to remove the obstacle of pride is to view it as the vicious enemy it is.

Come, everyone who is thirsty, come to
the waters; and you without money, come, buy,
and eat . . . without money and without cost.
Isaiah 55:1

God wants us to find our satisfaction
in Him alone rather than waste our time
and effort on things that cannot satisfy.
But I believe He creates and activates a
nagging dissatisfaction in us for an excellent reason, knowing full well that He has
created us with a need only He can meet.

He wants us to find the only thing that
will truly satiate our thirsty, hungry hearts.
Yet He gives us a will so we can choose
whether or not to accept His invitation to
"come" to Him. See, dissatisfaction is not
a terrible thing. It's a God-thing. It only
becomes a terrible thing when we don't let
it lead us to Christ.

Is there any God but Me?
There is no other Rock; I do not know any.
Isaiah 44:8

At some time each of us has exalted someone or something to a place where only God belonged. But to travel forward on the road to freedom, we must remove them from their places of inappropriate honor.

We begin by recognizing the obstacles as idol worship. (That's the easiest part.) But we may find removing them to be very difficult, because some of the idols in our lives have been in those places for years, and only the power of God can make them budge. Take heart in this, however: God is perfectly suited to displace every idol we possess and to set us free.

When the Spirit of truth comes,
He will guide you into all the truth.
John 16:13

Our craving to be filled is so strong that the moment something or someone seems to meet our need, we feel an overwhelming temptation to worship it. But if you are holding on to anything in your craving for satisfaction today, would you be willing to acknowledge it as a lie?

Even if you feel you can't let go of it right this moment, would you lift it before the Lord—perhaps literally lifting your fisted hand as a symbol—and confess it as an idol? The Holy Spirit does not convict you of this to condemn you but to help you become aware and seek forgiveness. Will you open your hand to Him? He is opening His to you.

So I discover this principle:
when I want to do good, evil is with me.
Romans 7:21

I can tell you from personal experience that at times of greatest captivity, I wanted nothing more than to be obedient to God. I was miserable in my rebellion, and I could not understand why I kept making wrong choices.

Yes, they were my choices, and I've taken full responsibility for them as my sins. But Satan had me in such a viselike grip, I felt powerless to obey, although I desperately wanted to. I *wasn't* powerless, of course, but as long as I believed the lie, I behaved accordingly. Sadly, I plunged to the depths before I discovered satisfaction in Him. I pray to settle for nothing less the rest of my days. Don't you?

Rejoice in hope; be patient in affliction;
be persistent in prayer.
Romans 12:12

What victory the enemy has in winning us over to prayerlessness! He would rather we do anything than pray.

He'd rather see us serve ourselves into the ground, because he knows we'll eventually grow resentful without prayer. He'd rather see us study the Bible into the wee hours of the morning, because he knows we'll never have both deep understanding and the power to live what we've learned without prayer. He knows prayerless lives are powerless lives—a sure prescription for anxiety, a certain way to avoid peace—while prayerful lives are powerful lives.

Devote yourselves to prayer;
stay alert in it with thanksgiving.
Colossians 4:2

One of the reasons why prayerlessness is such an obstacle is because when Satan takes aim at us, none of the following will help to keep us out of a snare if we're not in constant communication with God:

1) *Discipline*. At times of great temptation and weakness, discipline can fly like a bird out the nearest window.

2) *Past lessons*. We don't tend to think straight when we get a surprise attack.

3) *What is best for us*. Human nature is far too self-destructive to choose what is best at our weakest moments.

Prayer lets us walk in peace and victory even when walking through a war zone.

> . . . your feet sandaled with
> readiness for the gospel of peace.
> *Ephesians 6:15*

Our feet are our means of staying balanced as we stand. In this portion of Scripture on spiritual armor—where we learn about all the things God has given us in order to be alert and powerful in His Spirit—Paul talks about how our feet help us in battle.

Our balance out on the battlefield comes from knowing that, although we are definitely at war with Satan, who is admittedly powerful, we are at peace with God, who is gloriously omnipotent and fights our battles for us. Our feet are fitted for spiritual warfare when they are rested snugly in the gospel of peace.

Pray also for us that God may open a door
to us for the message, to speak the mystery of
the Messiah—for which I am in prison.
Colossians 4:3

Can you imagine how different the
apostle Paul's life and the life of the infant
church would have been if he had allowed
fear to rule him, if he had not depended
on prayer? Through faith—the opposite
of fear—Paul was spiritually loosed even
though he was physically chained. Had he
given way to fear, he may have been able
to remain physically loosed, but he would
have been spiritually chained.

Prayer matters. It's not just words in
the air. The Spirit of God released through
our prayers and the prayers of others is
enough to turn cowards into conquerors,
chaos into calm, cries into comfort.

My house will be called a house of prayer.
Isaiah 55:7

Abraham prayed. Isaac prayed. Jacob prayed. Moses left Pharaoh and prayed. Moses prayed for the people. Hannah wept much and prayed. David prayed. Elijah stepped forward and prayed. Job prayed for his friends. Hezekiah prayed to the Lord. Daniel got down on his knees and prayed. From inside the fish, Jonah prayed. Very early in the morning, while it was still dark, Jesus got up, left the house and went off to a solitary place, where He prayed. Going a little farther, He fell with His face to the ground and prayed.

Our enemy certainly knows the power of prayer. He's been watching it furiously for thousands of years.

Is there no balm in Gilead? Is there no physician there? So why has the healing of my dear people not come about?
Jeremiah 8:22

I sometimes ask people to take a look back at both the positives and negatives in their heritage, not to argue genetics versus environment, but to help them be loosed from anything hindering their lives with Christ.

Our enemy knows that issues left in shrouds of secrecy never get exposed to the healing light of God. You may recognize some ancient ruins in generations of your family. But thank God that, although you cannot change the past, He can help you change what you're doing with it. And the changes He makes in you in the present can certainly change your future!

Don't move an ancient property
line that your fathers set up.
Proverbs 22:28

An ancient boundary stone was much like a fence. It served as a visual reminder of what belonged to the landowner and what was beyond legal limits. It reminded people when they were crossing the line.

God's Ten Commandments, listed in Exodus 20, are the ultimate boundary stone. We are not free to move them around to fit our lifestyles. But there is a much more practical aspect to this than mere disobedience. Those who live beyond the boundaries will return to bondage. Not only will they return, they will leave a well-trodden path for the next generation to follow.

November

> You must not bow down
> to them or worship them; for I,
> the Lord your God, am a jealous God.
> *Exodus 20:5*

The idea of God's jealousy proves a stumbling block for some people. When God referred to Himself as a jealous God, He obviously wasn't jealous of idols. They possess no glory and can offer no salvation. All that idols can do is detract attention from the one true God, the One worthy of our praise, our only Deliverer.

God's jealousy is more like that of a parent whose child has become entangled in a destructive cult. This mom or dad will work and pray tirelessly until that child is restored to freedom. The parent is not jealous *of* her but *for* her. God is like that—jealous for us, His children.

The great dragon was thrown out—the ancient
serpent, who is called the Devil and Satan,
the one who deceives the whole world.
Revelation 12:9

The "ancient serpent" has been around
a long time. We can safely assume he and
his cohorts know more about our family
heritage than the most extensive genea-
logical research could uncover. Truly, if
knowledge is power, our enemy is pretty
powerful—and has no qualms with using
our earthly heritage to lead us astray.

In spite of thousands of years of existence, however, I don't think the ancient
serpent has a wealth of new ideas. He
probably tries the same general lure on us
that he used on those who came before us
in our family lines. Not very creative,
maybe, but highly effective. What are the
obvious things he keeps trying on you?

Don't let anyone deceive you in any way.
2 Thessalonians 2:3

Satan is a deceiver, leading our minds astray. He is both cunning and subtle, and the more undetected his work remains, the less we'll be able to resist him. One of the great dangers of a generational yoke, for example, is that it blends in so well with the rest of our lives and families.

One day, we were walking our dog on a trail in the country, when Keith suddenly grabbed me and said, "Don't move!" The biggest copperhead he had ever seen was curled up on the path just a few feet in front of us. Keith saw the snake because he was a hunter. He has an eye for camouflaged creatures. So should we.

If anyone suffers as a Christian, he should not be ashamed, but should glorify God with that name.

1 Peter 4:16

Part of finding wholeness is coming to terms with our family heritage Christ's way. In Him, we can take the best and leave the worst behind. We need to love and accept family members even though we may not always approve of their life-styles or spend lots of time together. Even if unity is not possible, we need the peace Christ can bring.

For liberty to be a reality, we need to be free of wrongdoing, even if no one else in the family follows suit. If this is an issue in your family, begin praying about it in a renewed way, asking God for the freedom to follow Him faithfully through this.

If only my request would be granted
and God would provide what I hope for.
Job 6:8

When I began to seek wholeness in Christ, I finally mustered the courage to ask Him where I was most vulnerable. He revealed to me that I feared having no one to take care of me; and if I didn't let Him heal that part of me, I would be vulnerable to unhealthy relationships.

God and I worked very hard on this issue, and I am so glad we did. Although my parents have been wonderful and my husband is an excellent provider, the reality is this: God is my only guarantee. The Knower of all my needs is also the sole Meeter of my needs. Only He can wholly and fully provide.

Sin will not rule over you, because you
are not under law but under grace.

Romans 6:14

Perhaps you come from an unusually
healthy family. On the other hand, you
may have descended from the opposite
extreme and see nothing positive in your
lineage. I pray that you will let God shed
a little light on the shades of grace and
goodness in your heritage.

Probably, however, you are a lot like
me—a blend of the best and worst of your
earthly lineage. I pray you'll ask God to
help you discern the difference and allow
Him to break all negative bonds. I know
you want to pass down the very best to
your children, both physical and spiritual.
In straining ahead for an ideal, you are
sure to reach positive change.

> They will rebuild the ancient ruins;
> they will restore the former devastations.
> *Isaiah 61:4*

"They" in this passage referred to the Israelite captives who had been set free. But I believe we can apply figuratively to ourselves what applied to them literally. Just as God appointed the Israelites to rebuild the wall of Jerusalem, He appoints us to rebuild our ancient ruins. He assigns to us the role of reconstruction worker.

I believe one reason why God requires our cooperation is that He deeply desires our involvement with Him. He created us for this purpose. Rebuilding ancient ruins is impossible for us without God. But as we draw near to Him, He rebuilds our lives and characters. He heals us by giving us relationship with Himself.

We must not hide them from
their children, but must tell a future
generation the praises of the Lord.

Psalm 78:4

Every generation has a new opportunity to exert positive influence. No matter what atrocity has taken place in your family line, God can raise up a new generation and turn the wheels of the cycle in the direction of godly seed.

Your great-grandfather could serve a life sentence for murder, and yet your own grandchild could serve a life sentence of faithful evangelism through which thousands come to know Christ. If your dream or desire for your grandchildren and great-grandchildren is in keeping with what you know of God's will, then you have the endorsement and approval of Christ to begin acting on it.

. . . showing faithful love
to a thousand generations of those who
love Me and keep My commands.
Exodus 20:6

The Hebrew word for "showing" in this verse means "to construct, to build." Right there in the context of generational influence, God promises to build blessing on the lives of those who love Him and obey Him.

The Ancient of Days is anxiously waiting to build a solid foundation that your descendants can live on for years to come if they choose. If you do your part for one generation, He'll do His for a thousand. I don't know how much longer Christ will tarry, but I don't expect Him to linger a thousand generations. That means your life could affect every generation until He comes. Isn't that worth it?

Insults have broken my heart, and I am in despair. I waited for sympathy, but there was none; for comforters, but found no one.

Psalm 69:20

Have these words ever described your heart? Has your heart felt as if wild beasts were fighting over it? Can you remember one particular moment when, figuratively speaking, you felt your heart break? Did you have any idea at the time that God cared so much that He aimed His Son straight at your heart?

Are you in bondage to a broken heart you have never let Christ bind and heal? Would you be willing to expose your heart one more time, just to Him? After all, this is what His Father sent Him to do. The bow has been stretched and the Arrow is ready. It's up to you to drop your shield.

God is not a God of disorder but of peace.
1 Corinthians 14:33

Christ is never the author of abuse, even though the Bible teaches us that some hardships are specifically ordained by God for the purpose of our personal growth and refining.

Child abuse is not one of them.

When you're trying to discern whether God or Satan is the author of a hardship, one of your best clues is to look and see whether sin was involved. God never entices us to sin, nor does He employ sin or perversion as a means of molding us into the image of Christ. Impossible! He may allow it, but He does not employ it.

I call to God Most High,
to God who fulfills His purpose for me.
Psalm 57:2

Among other things, I believe some of the reasons why God allowed childhood victimization to happen to me were:

1) To help me have compassion toward people who have been hurt in childhood.

2) He knew that the crime of childhood victimization would "come out of the closet" in this generation, and His desire was to call forth Christian spokespeople to address it from His Word.

3) He wanted me to teach how to make freedom in Christ a reality in life from the passion of personal experience.

He always has His reasons.

Lord, You see the wrong done to me.

Lamentations 3:59

If you have been the victim of abuse, you may be thinking, "The complications and repercussions of this are so overwhelming. It's just so hard to deal with!" I agree. That's one of the reasons why it would be better for any victimizer "if a heavy millstone were hung around his neck and he were drowned in the depths of the sea!" (Matt. 18:6).

Undoubtedly, childhood victimization is a major giant to battle throughout life, especially if the perpetrator was someone who was supposed to protect you. But just as surely as God empowered young David to slay Goliath, He'll empower you if you will let Him.

Whenever you stand praying, if you have
anything against anyone, forgive him.
Mark 11:25

Forgiving my perpetrator didn't mean
suddenly shrugging my shoulders, mutter-
ing, "Okay, I forgive," and going on as if
things hadn't happened. They *did* happen.
And they took a terrible toll on my life.

But forgiveness involved my handing
over to God the responsibility for justice.
The longer I held on to it, the more the
bondage strangled the life out of me.
Forgiveness meant my deferring the cause
to Christ and deciding to be free of the
ongoing burden of bitterness and blame. I
guess I just came to the point where I felt
more sorry for him than I did for me. I'd
rather be the loved and cherished victim
than the victimizer.

Then He showed me Joshua the high priest
standing before the Angel of the Lord, with Satan
standing at his right side to accuse him.

Zechariah 3:1

Isn't the enemy's gain one more reason
why we must refuse to let him have
another inch of ground over something in
our past? It's time to direct our indigna-
tion toward the author of abuse: Satan
himself. Ultimately, the accuser (Satan) is
the main abuser.

I was abused more times than I would
like to count, but Satan accused me every
day of my life from that time on until I
finally said, "Enough!" and agreed to let
God bring healing and forgiveness. We
must not be defined by anything that has
happened to us or anything we have done.
We are defined by who we are in Christ.

I chose you before I formed you in the womb;
I set you apart before you were born.

Jeremiah 1:5

"My Child, I knew every difficulty you would face in life. I suffered each one with you. I loved you and had a plan for your life before you were born. This plan has not changed, no matter what happened or what you have done.

"See, I knew all things concerning you before I formed you, and I would never allow any hurt to come into your life that I could not use for eternity. *Will you let Me?* Your truth will be incomplete unless you view it against the backdrop of my truth. Your story will remain half-finished until you let Me do my half with your hurt. Let Me perfect that which concerns you. I remain, your Faithful Father."

> But my eyes look to You,
> Lord God. I seek refuge in You.
> *Psalm 141:8*

We can't always count on sympathy from others when our hearts are suddenly shattered. Our heartbreaks aren't really anyone else's responsibility. In reality, they belong to Jesus.

Remember, He came to bind up the brokenhearted. All anyone can really do is sit with us and watch our heart bleed, because they can only take that kind of intimacy for a short period of time! But Jesus is never intimidated by the depth of our need and the demonstration of our weakness. I am so glad I don't have to keep a stiff upper lip when I'm all alone with God and hurting. Aren't you?

For we do not have a high priest who is
unable to sympathize with our weaknesses.

Hebrews 4:15

What sinful or hurtful things have you
either done or wanted to do? If I'm reading this verse correctly, Christ was also
tempted to react just like you were. I find
great comfort in knowing Christ doesn't
throw His hand over His mouth in shock
when I wish I could act a certain way.

And yet He has met our same temptations without sin. That encourages me.
No matter how I have reacted to betrayal
or any other kind of heartbreak in the
past, I am so glad to know that a way
exists to be victorious. Christ has already
done it! And if I follow Him through my
situation, I too can do it. It's never too late
to start following His lead in a crisis.

> Everyone who lives and believes in Me
> will never die—ever. Do you believe this?
> *John 11:26*

Death seems so final. Even if we believe that death is not the end, our hearts often lag far behind. But all believers in Christ will rise from the dead. He never allows any illness to end in death for a Christian. Please don't think me morbid, but I'm not sure Lazarus got the better end of the deal! When I die, I would rather not wake up and do it all over again!

But just as death is never the end of anyone's life in Christ, neither does it have to be the end for the loved one who is left behind. Do you feel like you can hardly go on living? Christ desires to raise you from the living dead.

In her chamber, the royal daughter is all glorious, her clothing embroidered with gold.

Psalm 45:13

If Satan has convinced you to see yourself as anything less than the handpicked child of the King of kings . . . if you think anything could happen to steal your royal heritage . . . if you think you deserve mistreatment or disrespect, then you have something in common with King David's daughter Tamar and all of those whose womanhood has been victimized.

I pray that the Holy Spirit will mend the torn coats of the children of royalty. I pray that He will restore lost dignity, teach us our true identity, and liberate us to live in purity. Having your clothing "embroidered with gold," dear sister in Christ, is your destiny.

You have captured my heart,
my sister, my bride.
Song of Songs 4:9

Interestingly, God's Word doesn't refer to us as *wives* of Christ but as the bride. To me, the word *bride* indicates lots of things *wife* doesn't. *Bride* implies newness and freshness. A crisp, beautiful dress. The fragrance of perfume. Richly colored lips. Sparkling eyes. I usually picture youthfulness. Perhaps innocence.

I believe all of these things will characterize our relationship with Christ and the ultimate consummation of our marriage. Scripture implies that our relationship to Christ, though enduring for an eternity, will ever remain fresh and true. Somehow, we will always be brides.

> I remember the loyalty of
> your youth, your love as a bride—
> how you followed Me in the wilderness.
>
> *Jeremiah 2:2*

One of the characteristics of a loving bride is her willingness to follow the groom to places that at times may seem like a wilderness. Our Bridegroom does sometimes lead us to difficult places, but we can trust Him to always have purpose in our stay and to never forsake us.

Usually, the reason our earthly groom moves us to new places is to seek a higher quality of life. I believe the same is true of Christ. All the moves He prompts are to give us a better quality of life. Even when we follow Him into the wilderness, seeking Him more frequently than ever, He allows us to experience His fulfillment.

He is the radiance of His glory,
the exact expression of His nature, and He
sustains all things by His powerful word.
Hebrews 1:3

When I was preparing for my wedding, I often thought about being a wife. Not just any wife. Keith's wife. The same is true as we prepare to be eternal brides. We won't just be part of a beautiful ceremony. We will be the bride of Christ.

God's Word doesn't imply that we are to make ourselves ready merely for the wedding but for the Groom. Thus, we cannot make ourselves ready without thinking about Him—meditating on our similarities (which hopefully are multiplying), thinking about our differences and how we might adjust, simply thinking about how wonderful He is!

My God will supply all your needs according
to His riches in glory in Christ Jesus.

Philippians 4:19

The enemy is an expert archer. And
when women are the target, the bull's-eye
is often childhood dreams.

We grew up believing in Cinderella,
yet some of us feel our palace turned out
to be a duplex, our prince turned out to be
a frog, and the wicked stepmother turned
out to be our mother-in-law. Our fairy
godmother apparently lost our address.

Yet it's true that many of our childhood dreams were meant to come true
only in Christ—in ways far grander than
the obvious. God sometimes allows us to
be disappointed so we will set our hopes
more fully in Him.

A man's wisdom brightens his face,
and the sternness of his face is changed.

Ecclesiastes 8:1

One of the grandest miracles that comes from having a wonderful, fulfilling relationship with Christ *now* instead of waiting until heaven is the stress He can relieve from other relationships.

Loving Christ does not cause me to love my husband less. On the contrary, through Christ I love him more. Christ helps us see each other more like He sees us. He takes up the slack in our imperfect relationship and reminds us that the ideal partnership is ahead. Until then, our challenges simply help us grow and prepare for eternity. Being beautiful to Christ frees me to look and be my best without feeling the bondage to look and be better.

My Father is glorified by this: that you produce
much fruit and prove to be My disciples.
John 15:8

God created every life to be fruitful
and multiply, but this God-given dream
represents more than physical offspring. I
believe our dream to have babies represents a desire to have fruitful lives, to
invest ourselves in something that matters,
something that makes a difference. Our
disappointment with God is often the
result of our small thinking.

The potential for spiritual offspring—
those we can teach and help and grow up
in the faith—is virtually limitless in the
lives and hearts of the physically barren. If
God restricts you from physical offspring,
He desires to empower you to bear spiritual offspring, to bear much fruit.

Share your master's joy!
Matthew 25:21

Each of us has dreams. And if we trust Christ with all our hearts, nothing can disable God from surpassing our dreams with His divine reality.

The suicide of her husband could not keep God from surpassing Kay Arthur's dreams. Sudden paralysis could not keep God from surpassing Joni Eareckson Tada's dreams. A horrifying ordeal in a Nazi concentration camp could not keep God from surpassing Corrie ten Boom's dreams. God surpasses our dreams when we reach past our personal plans and agendas to grab the hand of Christ and walk the path He has chosen for us.

They are rebellious people,
deceitful children, children unwilling
to listen to the Lord's instruction.

Isaiah 30:9 (NIV)

The Hebrew word for "listen" in this verse is *shama*, meaning "to give undivided listening attention." Are you like me? Do you have difficulty giving anyone your undivided attention? Isaiah 30:9, however, doesn't describe the accidentally inattentive. The truth is, rebellious people don't *want* to listen.

Sometimes we won't listen to God because we're resistant to being corrected, redirected, or challenged to change. But the tragedy is that God would never tell us anything to defeat us. He has a one-track mind as far as we're concerned. He wants us to live like the overcomers we are.

I called to the Lord in distress; the Lord
answered me and put me in a spacious place.

Psalm 118:5

In returning to God and resting confidently in His promises and power, we will
continually find salvation. The Hebrew
word for "salvation" is *yasha*, meaning
"to be open, wide, or free . . . It is the
opposite of *tsarar*, to cramp." This word
draws the picture of a spacious place in
which to move.

I've personally experienced the wide-
open freedom of obedience to Christ, but
I've also known the miserable, pinned-in
feeling of rebellion. Returning to the Lord
is not a matter of determining to do better
in our own strength, but of letting Him
place us Himself in the roomy spaces of
His love and grace.

> Pharaoh's protection will become your shame,
> and refuge in Egypt's shadow your disgrace.
> *Isaiah 30:3*

What happens if we continue in rebellion, rejecting God's Word, relying on oppression, and depending on deceit? The figurative walls of protection around our lives will crumble like pottery broken to pieces. Those who are Christians will not lose salvation, but we stand to lose a significant amount of protection.

As I've said before, the bottom line is this: clay that insists on acting like the Potter will inevitably end up in pieces. Thank goodness, though, that God still loves cracked pots! Let's not wait until we're in pieces to return to Him, trusting in His power to heal and protect.

December

God is enthroned above the circle of the earth.
Isaiah 40:22

If you spend much time in Isaiah 40, you discover some powerful statements on God's superiority over creation, idols, and humanity, as well as His absolute uniqueness.

• He is able to measure the waters in "the hollow of His hand" (v. 12).
• Idols are not only a long way from being godly but are man-made (v. 19).
• No human being can understand or instruct Him or give Him counsel (v. 13).
• "Who is My equal?" (v. 25).

Never expect to approach His Word without being sobered and humbled once again at His greatness.

> But My salvation will last forever,
> and My righteousness will never be shattered.
> *Isaiah 51:6*

Every one of us creatures who have cast ourselves on God's mercy can know for certain that His righteousness will never fail, nor will *we* fail when we choose to obey Him. His righteousness will last forever, and so will we, because He credits our belief with eternal righteousness.

Yes, the same Lord who is our Maker is also our Defender. Our oppressor will one day cower at His feet. The God who churns up the sea can also make a road in its depths so that we may cross over. The One who set the heavens in place and laid the foundations of the earth covers us with the shadow of His hand.

Therefore we will not be afraid,
though the earth trembles and the mountains
topple into the depths of the seas.
Psalm 46:2

What one thing does every human being on earth need? What do we need when our mountains shake? When our hills are removed?

Babies die without it. Children require it. Youth plead for it with their words and actions. Adults spend their lives searching for it.

Everybody needs to be loved with a love that will never fail or go away. Truly, our hearts will never be healthy unless we learn to accept, receive, and abide in God's unfailing love.

God, who is abundant in mercy,
because of His great love that He had for us,
made us alive with the Messiah.

Ephesians 2:4–5

God's love impacted the lives of many key people in Scripture. Moses penned his conviction that God in His unfailing love would lead His people to His "holy dwelling" (Exod. 15:13). David wrote that "the one who trusts in the Lord will have faithful love surrounding him" (Ps. 32:10).

Even after the destruction of Jerusalem, Jeremiah recognized that "even if He causes suffering, He will show compassion according to His abundant, faithful love" (Lam. 3:32). A child of God who believes she is loved is sure to experience the wholeness found only in Christ.

> Be gracious to me, God, according to Your
> faithful love; according to Your abundant
> compassion, blot out my rebellion.
>
> *Psalm 51:1*

How important is the link between the love of God and the mercy of God? Oh beloved, please receive this truth—the Father cannot be unbiased toward you. He cannot set His love aside and make a cold, objective decision. Once you become God's covenant child by receiving His Son as your Savior, He cannot see you through anything less than a loving Father's eyes.

You and I will never be rejected when we come to Him with genuine hearts of repentance, ready to fall into His loving arms. Remember, Christ was never resistant to sinners in the Gospel accounts. He was only resistant to hypocrites.

In Your faithful love destroy my enemies.
Wipe out those who attack me,
for I am Your servant.
Psalm 143:12

What a secure, comforting level of rest God's unfailing love affords us when an enemy rises up against us! Do you realize that if our hearts are humble and right before God, we can hand over to Him all the conflicts and foes that rise up against us, knowing that He will deal with them in His own holy and just way?

What happens if we, too, were in the wrong? What if our foe had good reason to set himself in opposition to us? We must certainly do everything we can to apologize and make things right, but if the foe remains against us, he or she is God's responsibility, not ours.

Be steadfast, immovable, always excelling
in the Lord's work, knowing that your
labor in the Lord is not in vain.
1 Corinthians 15:58

Have you noticed how two people can look at the same experience differently? Recall a crisis in your home. Perhaps a number of people were affected, but you probably noticed how different the reactions and responses were. You see, each person's mind worked differently to frame the situation.

Often we cause ourselves more pain by the way we frame events than the events themselves cause. That's why, whenever temptations and troubling thoughts arise, steadfast believers lay their hands on God's Word and know that it's the truth. They frame life by the truth of the Bible.

Yet God drags away the mighty by His power;
when He rises up, they have no assurance of life.
Job 24:22

We have an uncanny way of rational-
izing the strongholds that possess us, the
ones we allow to continue in our lives.
You've had them. I've had them. But never
forget that Satan persists wherever a
stronghold exists. He always supplies an
endless list of rationalizations for the
things we do and refuse to do.

Can you think of a rationalization or
excuse that no longer has power over you?
If so, never forget that the same God who
came to your aid before will come to your
aid again! You may feel like your present
obstacles are larger, but I assure you, God
doesn't. He is all-powerful!

For as heaven is higher than earth,
so My ways are higher than your ways,
and My thoughts than your thoughts.

Isaiah 55:9

Many of our mammoth captors began as seeds in the thought life, but we watered and cultivated them by continued meditation until they grew to the size of Sequoias! Other times, sudden unwelcome or overwhelming circumstances cause full-grown trees to appear. But no matter whether these captors of ours began as seeds or trees, their destructive force assumes the size they occupy in our mind.

Securing a steadfast mind, then, is not a matter of denial. Rather, it begins with admitting the truth. Then with our willing cooperation, God begins to strip the power from these controlling thoughts so they no longer hold destructive power over us.

Therefore, make a confession to the
Lord God of your fathers and do His will.
Ezra 10:11

Confession means coming to the point
of saying the same thing God says about
any specific matter. For the believer, the
first step of freedom from any stronghold
is agreeing with God concerning the
personal sin involved.

Please understand, the object itself of
our imaginations is not always sin. The
sin may lie solely in the exaltation of it in
our own minds. For example, nothing
could be more reflective of the heart of
God than a mother's love for her child.
But if she passes the bounds of healthy
affection to overprotection, obsession,
and idolatry, she has constructed a stronghold. We can't be free until we confess it.

Look, the Devil is about to throw some of
you into prison to test you. . . . Be faithful until
death, and I will give you the crown of life.
Revelation 2:10

Once we are willing to see the sin that
is involved in our strongholds and agree
with God through confession, we begin to
see the lies surrounding us. It's in tearing
down these lies wallpapering our minds
that our prison doors swing open.

But while Satan does not possess the
power or authority to lock believers in
prisons of oppression, he does work over-
time to talk us into staying, having wooed
us there with all the lures he has perfected.
Unfortunately, he doesn't require a written invitation to do his dirty work. Our
failure to post a "keep away" sign through
Bible study and prayer can be an invitation by default.

Whoever is blessed in the land
will be blessed by the God of truth.
Isaiah 65:16

Once we tear down the wallpaper of lies on our prison walls, we must determine to put up truth in its place.

Give this next statement your full attention: *the walls of your mind will never stay bare.* Once you tear down lies, you must rewallpaper with truth, or the enemy will happily supply a new roll of his own. Different pattern, maybe—a more updated look—but the same old deceptive manufacturer.

I cannot emphasize this step enough. Truth is the only way to reprogram our way out of captivity.

The entirety of Your word is truth, and
all Your righteous judgments endure forever.
Psalm 119:160

Expect the battle to heat up when you start tearing down the lies in your mind. So be prepared to fight for your freedom with some radical choices.

In the heat of a particular battle of mine, I can remember a time when I took my spiral-bound collection of Scriptures (my "Truth Cards") into the grocery store with me. I put them in the baby seat, and every aisle or two, I would flip to the next card. Our cupboard was filled with the strangest concoction of stuff you've ever seen, but I'm free today! God's Word is your truth serum. The more you use it, the clearer your mind will become.

> The one who has My word should
> speak My word truthfully, for what
> is straw compared to grain?
> *Jeremiah 23:28*

Coming out from under the influence of a long-term stronghold can be like coming out from under the long-term influence of a drug. You'll often find that the magnitude of the stronghold takes a while to fathom. But the more you wake up to the truth, the more you'll realize that Satan has deceived you. It's not at all unusual to feel twice the regret several months after your release than you did when you first walked away.

Until you are less vulnerable, flood your mind with truth and with other materials that line up with truth (as opposed to the prevailing lies of the media and other deceptive influences).

The mind-set of the flesh is death,
but the mind-set of the Spirit is life and peace.
Romans 8:6

When we do not make the deliberate choice to think according the Spirit, we "default" to the flesh. You've noticed we never have to wake up in the morning and choose to be self-centered. We default into self-centeredness automatically unless we deliberately submit to the authority of Christ and the fullness of His free Spirit.

When we think according to the flesh, we are often anxious, unnerved, insecure, and fearful, not to mention greedy, lustful, jealous, and all sorts of things we were never meant to be as Christians. But even when the Holy Spirit convicts us of sin, His purpose is for life and peace. He edifies the believer. He doesn't tear us down.

Those who belong to Christ Jesus have
crucified the flesh with its passions and desires.
Galatians 5:24

Pray for God to give you a heightened
awareness of the way you're thinking. Try
to become alert to times when you're
thinking according to the flesh. Recognize
the feeling it is sowing in your heart.

I often hear people say, "I can't change
the way I feel. No, but we can change the
way we think, and that in turn will change
the way we feel. The less we feed the Spirit
of God within us with things that energize
Him to fill us, the more His presence will
"shrink" within us. But praise God, the
opposite is also true. The more we feed
the Spirit of God and yield to His control,
the more His presence will fill and satiate
us with life and peace.

They are the branch I planted, the work
of My hands, so that I may be glorified.
Isaiah 60:21

The entire goal of our journey toward
breaking free is wrapped up in bringing
glory to God. Christ came to set the
captives free so that we could be the
branches He "planted" in righteousness,
the "work" of His "hands."

Will others look on our lives and call
us displays of God's splendor? Maybe.
Often, however, we will find that others
won't understand our freedom and may
even despise us for what we've done and
where we've come from. We can't count
on others to always call us as God see us!
So who will look on the captives set free
and recognize at a glance the glories of
His presence in us? I believe God will.

> Blessed is the man who
> trusts in the Lord. . . . He will be
> like a tree planted by water.
> *Jeremiah 17:7–8*

Being a tree isn't so bad when you've been planted by the Lord for the express purpose of displaying His splendor. Like Moses, whose face shone with the glory of God in Exodus 34, the life of a captive set free radiates the splendor of God. Is it any wonder that this is so? Any captive who has victoriously made freedom in Christ a reality in life has spent more than a little time in the presence of God.

If you've agreed to go the extra mile with God and to do whatever freedom requires, you are someone God can boast about. He is so proud of you! You are a living, visible portrait of the enthralling beauty of God.

The Lamb who was slaughtered is worthy
to receive power and riches and wisdom and
strength and honor and glory and blessing!
Revelation 5:12

God chose one nation to be called by
His name, through whom He would bless
all other nations by bringing the Messiah.
The Israelites were literally a people of
God's name, called forth as a nation to
show the definite and conspicuous position of the one true God in their lives.

The name that you and I are called
most often in reference to our spiritual
belief is "Christian." We are a people of
Christ's name. Similarly, God has called
us to show the definite and conspicuous
position of His one and only Son in our
lives. We are called to bear the mark of
His individuality, to proclaim His honor,
authority, and character.

I long for You in the night; yes, my spirit
within me diligently seeks You.
Isaiah 26:9

Without a doubt, the more you know
God, the more you *want* to know God.
The more time you spend with Him, the
more you will yearn for Him.

The yearning described in Isaiah 26:9
comes from the heart and soul of a person
who has truly known God, someone who
can say, "I gaze on You in the sanctuary to
see Your strength and glory" (Ps. 63:2).

People who know God well want God
to be well-known. No one has to force a
person who is intimately acquainted with
God to be a living witness. On the contrary,
those who truly know His name (and all it
implies) always want His fame.

To the only God our Savior, through Jesus
Christ our Lord, be glory, majesty, power, and
authority before all time, now, and forever.
Jude 25

My motivation for Bible study and
prayer could be all about me, if I let it.

- "Fix my circumstances, Lord."
- "Use me powerfully, Lord."
- "Direct me today."
- "Make a way for me."
- "Make me successful, Lord."

If my motivation for relating to God is
what He can do for me, then a lust for His
power may grow, but a yearning for His
presence will not. God deeply desires to
hear our petitions, but His greatest joy is
to hear them flow from the mouths of
those who want Him more than anything
else He could give.

> If you know Me, you will also know
> My Father. From now on you do know
> Him and have seen Him.
> *John 14:7*

If knowing God is not your chief motivation for prayer and Bible study, the last thing I want you to feel is guilt. Creating awareness is my goal. Awareness is always the first step to freedom.

In fact, it was this very awareness that motivated me in my late twenties to begin asking God to give me a heart to love Him and to know Him more than anything in my life. I do not have either the words or the space to explain the transformation that has taken place through this petition. To this day, this is the most often repeated request I make of God on my own behalf. More than anything on earth, I pray to know Him.

I will judge the nation they serve, and afterwards
they will go out with many possessions.
Genesis 15:14

When God delivers His people, they
never have to escape by the skin of their
teeth! The Israelites were impoverished
slaves, but when God delivered them, they
left with the riches of the Egyptians.

What about you? Did you come out of
Egypt—out of your time of slavery—with
plunder from the enemy? Did you give the
enemy an offensive blow by allowing God
to bring you out of captivity twice the
person you were when you went in? What
God appropriated to the nation of Israel
in a tangible sense, we can apply in a spiritual sense. He wants to bring us out of
our times of captivity with "possessions."

In this way they plundered the Egyptians.
Exodus 12:36

You don't have to escape from your time of captivity with nothing to show for it. After all that the enemy has put you through, take your plunder! Let God bring you forth from your time of slavery with gold, silver, and costly stones—stronger than ever, in fact, because in your weakness God was strong—more of a threat to the kingdom of darkness than Satan ever dreamed you'd be!

Don't just reclaim the ground you've surrendered. God wants to enlarge your borders and teach you to possess land you never knew existed. Make the enemy pay for scheming against you so hatefully.

The God of peace be with all of you.
Romans 15:33

One of the benefits of our covenant relationship with God is to experience His peace—the peace of the incarnate Prince of Peace whose birth we celebrate today.

What might the peace of God look like in our souls at its most beautiful moment? When does peace become an eye-catching display of God's splendor? Peace is the fruit of righteousness, which is experienced as we are obedient to His commands. It is the product of abiding in the vine—the way by which the wine of joy flows through our lives. As you bow in worship today, may you find both peace and joy in the Child of promise.

You were like sheep going astray,
but you have now returned to the shepherd
and guardian of your souls.
1 Peter 2:25

While I was still a sinner, Christ died for me. He heard the groans of my self-imposed slavery, looked on my ugliness, and called this captive free. And was there plunder? You are staring it in the face this very moment. This book, for whatever it's worth, is nothing but plunder. Every line is what God allowed me to take from my seasons in Egypt's humiliation.

I deserved to be placed on a shelf and to simply live out my time patiently until the glory of heaven. Instead, God chose to teach me with the very things Satan had used to defeat me. How could I not pour my life back into God? He is the only reason I have survived, let alone thrived!

He will transform the body of our humble
condition into the likeness of His glorious body.
Philippians 3:21

How I pray that you are already aware
of the plunder you stole from the enemy
after God delivered you from your times
of slavery. Let God have your failures.
Surrender to Him your most dreadful
moments of captivity, your most humiliat-
ing defeats. God and God alone can use
them to make you twice the warrior you
ever dreamed you'd be.

Be like the Israelites, who reinvested
the plunder of the Egyptians by offering it
back to God—a God who can take a few
simple fish and loaves and multiply them
to feed thousands—a God of awesome
returns. Reinvest all the things you have
brought with you out of captivity!

Better to be lowly of spirit with the humble
than to divide plunder with the proud.
Proverbs 16:19

I remember being in an Indian village
where raw sewage was running only a few
feet from me as I spoke to four women
through an interpreter. I touched their
faces and told them they were beautiful,
that God saw them with great dignity and
honor. Like princesses. Within minutes,
four women had turned into many. They
wept, held on to me, and were willing to
do anything to receive such a Savior.

What did God use to provoke such a
bond between these women and me? An
acute memory of my own former emptiness and oppression. In their faces I saw
my own. And in His, I saw our only hope.
For all of us.

He has satisfied the hungry with good things
and sent the rich away empty.
Luke 1:53

Oh, how I pray that each of us will discover glorious satisfaction in Christ. But when it's the real thing, we must find a place to pour the overflow of our lives.

Captives who have truly been set free are undoubtedly the most compassionate people in the world. They don't see others as less than themselves, because they've lived a little of their own lives in the gutter, as well.

The satisfied soul is never a more beautiful display of God's splendor than when she is willing to empty herself for the lives and needs of others.

Because of Him I have suffered the loss
of all things and consider them filth,
so that I may gain Christ.
Philippians 3:8

The thought of having to fight our way through life is exhausting. Can you think of anything more arduous than waking up to win every day? I could probably do it about four days a week. The other three, I'd want to push the snooze button and go back to sleep. There's got to be a better way.

There is! God doesn't want our goal to merely be winning, but to be winning Christ. More than you seek to defeat the enemy, seek his foe! More than you seek victory, seek the Victor! Hang on to Him for dear life, because you can be sure the place He is going is to victory!

You are my hiding place;
You protect me from trouble. You surround
me with joyful shouts of deliverance.
Psalm 32:7

For just a moment, I don't want you to think about how far you have to go. I just want you to think about how far you've come as I pray Psalm 32:7 over you: "May God be your hiding place; may He protect you from trouble, and may He incline your spiritual ears to listen carefully while He surrounds you with joyful songs of deliverance."

I come down to my knees in your honor, as well as God's. You, my fellow sojourner, are a display of His splendor. May the Lord break each evil bond that enslaves you and shine His healing light of liberation on your face.